Unwrap
the
Gifts

PAUL L. COX
with JULIA PFERDEHIRT

CREATION
HOUSE
A STRANG COMPANY

Unwrap the Gifts by Paul L. Cox with Julia Pferdehirt
Published by Creation House
A Strang Company
600 Rinehart Road
Lake Mary, Florida 32746
www.creationhouse.com

This book or parts thereof may not be reproduced in any form, stored in a retrieval system, or transmitted in any form by any means—electronic, mechanical, photocopy, recording, or otherwise—without prior written permission of the publisher, except as provided by United States of America copyright law.

Unless otherwise noted, all Scripture quotations are from the Holy Bible, New International Version. Copyright © 1973, 1978, 1984, International Bible Society. Used by permission.

Scripture quotations marked NKJV are from the New King James Version of the Bible. Copyright © 1979, 1980, 1982 by Thomas Nelson, Inc., publishers. Used by permission.

Scripture quotations marked NRSV are from the New Revised Standard Version of the Bible. Copyright © 1989 by the Division of Christian Education of the National Council of the Churches of Christ in the USA. Used by permission.

Scripture quotations marked NAS are from the New American Standard Bible. Copyright © 1960, 1962, 1963, 1968, 1971, 1972, 1973, 1975, 1977 by the Lockman Foundation. Used by permission. (www.Lockman.org)

Design Director: Bill Johnson
Cover design by Amanda Potter

Copyright © 2008 by Paul L. Cox
All rights reserved

Library of Congress Control Number: 2008926035
International Standard Book Number: 978-1-59979-384-9

08 09 10 11 12 — 987654321
Printed in the United States of America

This book is dedicated to my grandchildren:
Julianne Nicole Cox, Christopher Michael Cox,
Jessica Noel Lisle, Cody Andrew Lisle,
Amber Mikana-Aloha Cochran, Ethan Matieo Cochran
and Aaron Matthew Cochran.

May what has represented a new and unusual move
of the Spirit in my generation become normal for
you as you go and possess the land as the Joshua
generation.

AUTHOR'S NOTE

S PIRITUAL GIFTS CANNOT be easily defined or categorized. For example, what constitutes prophecy in one situation may be a word of knowledge in another. In this book, definitions are used primarily to help people in prayer ministry identify, understand, and use their gifts more effectively.

In personal narratives, most names and other details have been changed to ensure confidentiality.

CONTENTS

PROLOGUE

I N 1989 MY wife, Donna, and I lived as a Bible-believing, conservative pastor and his supportive spouse, sharing and ministering together. My preaching brought well-planned, substantive sermons to our congregation. We had a thriving church and beautiful kids. Life truly was wonderful.

However, John Wimber and the Vineyard Church movement were changing the Christian landscape in our Southern California community. Teaching about signs and wonders and whispers of miraculous healings penetrated even the theological walls of our American Baptist church. Members of the congregation began to ask questions. Donna and I and our entire church were about to hit a bump in our *wonderful* road.

As I read about Wimber and the Vineyard movement, my preconceptions began to crumble. I had expected to find a biblically unsound group of off-the-wall, radical people. Instead, I found clear, scriptural teaching and a call to take the Lord at His Word—literally. These "radicals" sounded like Baptists! As Baptists, we believe in teaching the Bible. If the Bible says it, we believe it.

I was more than curious; I felt challenged to embrace God's Word regardless of where it took me. That is a very dangerous thing to do. I prayed, "Lord, do with me what You want." I had no idea what I was doing or where it would lead.

In response to questions from the congregation, I scheduled a short sermon series on spiritual warfare in the fall of 1989.

I gathered books, tapes, and articles for study, intending to settle the issue and return to business as usual. The bump in the road was soon to become a roller coaster.

After my third sermon in the spiritual warfare series, a woman approached me and said, "That's me. What you're talking about—that's my problem." I listened carefully. As her story unfolded it became apparent that, at best, this woman was spiritually confused. At worst, she was plagued by demons. The issue of spiritual warfare, it seemed, could not be settled with a few sermons. The following Saturday the woman entered my office, accompanied by the one intercessor we had in the church. I had written down everything I knew about dealing with demons.

I started praying and asked the Lord to reveal what was going on. For twenty minutes nothing happened, but pretty soon a strange look came over the lady's face. "They're repeating everything you say," she said.

"Who's repeating?" I asked.

"The voices inside."

As we continued to pray, the woman's hands began to shake, and a voice unlike her own came from her mouth. The Lord drew out a memory of her being molested as a child.

At that point, we came face to face with a demon. It started saying, "You can't do anything about it." However, the woman forgave the person who had molested her, and when she told the demon to leave, it left. Another demon showed up, and it left.

That woman walked out the door a different person, and I left my office that day knowing that something had changed for myself, my ministry, and my understanding of spiritual warfare. I remember telling Donna, "Well, we made contact. Now what?"

Chapter One

THE ARENA OF SPIRITUAL WARFARE

C HRISTINA AND JOHN were church-going Christians when they received the news that Christina's brother, Rob, had been in a terrible traffic accident. They clung to each other and prayed while Rob was losing a battle with death two thousand miles away.

After pacing and praying for more than twenty-four hours, Christina collapsed into an exhausted, uneasy sleep. Long before she should have wakened, she entered a deep dream. Even in sleep, it was so real—and so absolutely beyond her life experience—that she recalled every detail. She told us about it when she came to Aslan's Place, the prayer ministry Donna and I lead, one year later.

"I was sleeping and my brother came to me," Christina said. "He lay down on the bed next to me and began to talk, asking me how Mom was taking it. I asked if he was going to be all right. Would he live? He answered that he hadn't been told yet. This was so real. So vivid. I sensed that it *was* real."

Some details seemed odd to Christina, even in her dream. "My mother had moved just weeks before to a house Rob had never seen. In the dream, Rob told me he had tried to find my mother and couldn't find her house, so he came to me.

"I tried to keep him there, asking him questions, wanting to know if he would live. It was as if I were trying to keep him alive by keeping him there.

"He talked for some time, then sat up. 'I have to go now, but I have something for you,' he said. He put what appeared to be a small, blue slip of paper in my hands. But as soon as I grasped it, it felt like a cord or a rope. I gripped the cord in my hands and begged him not to go. I remember being so afraid he would die and I would never see him again.

"I wouldn't let go of the cord, so he finally pulled away so suddenly and with such strength that I was thrown to the floor. He walked out the door, and I woke up on the floor with my hands clenched, as if I were still holding that cord."

Shaking and exhausted, Christina fumbled for pen and paper and recorded every detail of the strange, puzzling dream. What she could not have known was that while she was dreaming, Rob was dead; his heartbeat had ceased. In an operating room halfway across the country, skilled physicians were working desperately to bring him back from death using powerful drugs and twenty-first-century medical technology.

The next morning, as Christina and her mother scrambled to pack clothes, confirm airline tickets, and meet the outgoing flight to Rob's home city, Christina played and re-played the strange dream in her mind.

"I kept sensing that it was real," she recalled. "At that time, angels and near-death experiences were topics in magazines and on television. But nobody in our little town would believe my experience." Christina struggled to describe her dream to a few family members. "How could I tell other people about it when I wasn't sure what had really happened myself?" she questioned.

At the hospital, Christina and her family kept vigil for fifteen days while Rob lay in a deep coma. *Crash cart* and *Code*

Blue became familiar terms, and doctors gently prepared the family for Rob's death.

But Rob didn't die. On day fifteen, Christina sat beside him during the few minutes allowed to visitors each hour. "They finally pulled the breathing tube out so he could talk," she remembered. As she talked to him, she said, "I think I had a visit from you while I was sleeping."

Without a pause, Rob answered her, "Yes, you did," and then repeated their conversation—exactly.

Christina's mind whirled with questions. The whole, amazing dream must have been real. But how? What had happened? And what was the blue cord Rob had given her? She would wait months and even years for answers to most of her questions, but Rob knew one answer from that very moment. The blue cord was somehow related to him and to Christina's act of hanging on to him.

During the next months Rob healed, working daily to regain strength in his damaged body. Christina and John returned to their home in the Rocky Mountains, but for Christina, nothing was the same.

Christina launched a quest to learn about near-death experiences and read everything she could find on the topic. One subject led to another, and soon she had a small library of books about angels, spirit travel, life-after-death accounts, and communication with the deceased.

However, she found the church surprisingly silent on the matter. "I'd never heard anything like this mentioned in church. I drove miles to a Christian bookstore looking for some help, but couldn't find a single book. Secular books and TV were the only sources of information." Soon, Christina was taping episodes of *The Other Side*, a television program that featured stories of life-after-death experiences and communication with deceased loved ones.

It was then that the "other side" that Christina was trying to understand re-entered her life. "I had communication with what I thought was an angel," Christina said. "The angel was a comfort, and I felt care coming from it. It came to me first with words in my spirit, speaking in my mind." Christina grew to depend on "her angel." The spirit being told her its name, and soon she called upon it for help and comfort.

Thus began a time of confusion, pain, and physical and spiritual harassment that would take Christina into a downward spiral, like a plane in a fatal nosedive. Chaos took over her mind and spirit. Christina began seeing ugly creatures and hearing voices. She was repeatedly physically attacked, hit, and bitten. Red marks appeared on her body although nothing physical had touched her. Prayer and her guardian angel's presence were Christina's only shelter in this spiritual storm.

"Eventually, the only way I could sleep was to listen to Scripture put to music. However, the tape player kept going dead. I'd put new batteries in it, and it would die again. A deep voice, like a growl, came over the headphones and told me, 'You will not listen to this tape.'

"I was afraid nobody would believe me or they would assume that I was mentally ill. It was affecting my marriage. The more I tried to read books to understand what was happening to me, the more harassment I experienced. My husband felt so helpless."

THE BATTLE FOR CHRISTINA'S FREEDOM

For a year Christina fought a losing battle. Finally, in desperation, she contacted her new pastor, hoping that this virtual stranger might believe her but knowing he might just as easily decide she was mentally ill. The pastor met with John and Christina. As Christina came to realize, "This was God-ordained. He sent this pastor to our little town to tell me where to get help."

Christina left the meeting with a name, a phone number, and a thread of hope. She clung to all three as the weekend crawled by, and the next week, trembling, she called Aslan's Place and poured out her terrible story to me. That day, and for many days afterward, I prayed for Christina over the phone. For the first time Christina found hope. The battle had begun. Initial prayer brought some relief—small changes, such as being able to sleep, which seemed like miracles to Christina and John. Soon they scheduled a trip to California to meet Donna and me face to face at Aslan's Place, where teams of mature Christians commonly assemble to pray for hurting, wounded people.

Our prayer team members bring unique spiritual gifting and insight to the ministry at each prayer session. Some intercessors may hear the Lord speak words of instruction or direction, either audibly or in his or her spirit. Others may receive images or mental pictures. God may give visions or reveal information unknown to anyone but the person who is receiving prayer. The Lord may also reveal His mind, will, and intention to prayer teams through specific words or Scriptures, emotions, thoughts, and physical manifestations. These may be expressed through touch, temperature, smell, sight, and hearing.

Following my leadership, team members prayed and waited for the Lord's direction and revelation as we began our ministry to Christina on her first visit. I had been praying for peace and protection from demonic attack, and now the battle for Christina's life, peace, and spiritual freedom escalated. The team, which included a prayer minister named Janelle, wanted to find and remove the roots of the bondage Christina was experiencing.

"Christina had a special relationship with her angel," Janelle later recalled. "I felt this 'check' in my spirit, like the Lord was saying, 'Slow down. Pay attention here. Something isn't right.'"

As Janelle prayed and asked the Lord to show her the truth about Christina's situation, she searched her memory for any scriptural example of humans having relationships with angels. "It just didn't sit right with the Scriptures," she realized. Janelle began to feel what she describes as a creeping fear. In the past she had experienced that same sensation, sometimes coupled with the sight of flickering lights, when evil was present.

"Lord, who is this angel?" Janelle prayed silently. As she prayed, she had a visual image of a leather strap around Christina's neck. In that moment her mind cleared and she knew with certainty that God had answered her request for the truth.

As Christina describes it, "Janelle said that my guardian angel was really a demon that had me in bondage. I wondered, was that the leather strap I had been feeling around my neck?" For many months, Christina had been plagued by a physical pressure "like a heavy crown or weight" on her head, and now it felt as if screws in the side of her head were being turned, tighter and tighter.

Christina cringed. "How could that be my guardian angel? It can't be," she thought. "He told me his name."

"Ask the Lord to show you the truth," I said. "Ask if this guardian angel is wearing a mask."

Christina felt frozen. Immobilized. Conflicting thoughts circled in her mind like boxers in a ring. How could she doubt the angel that had been her companion and comfort? The questions about her angel seemed fabricated and ridiculous. Hadn't she heard that Christians couldn't have demons?

For twenty minutes or more, Christina sat in silent struggle. "I was so hurting, so desperate. Finally I told the angel to go to Jesus and asked Jesus to show me the truth. I closed my eyes and said, 'In the name of Jesus Christ, drop your mask if you are a deceiver.'" Instantly, the beautiful face turned into a hideous, ugly demon. Christina's friend, companion, and guardian angel was actually a demonic, "familiar" spirit.

Christina's complete freedom wasn't won in a single battle. This was a war, with still more ground to take. Between prayer sessions, the prayer team and Christina asked Jesus for understanding. She learned that the visit by her brother was real. Although communicating with her brother in the dream wasn't sinful in itself, Christina soon understood that she had clung to Rob as she clung to the blue cord. She also saw clearly how her efforts to make sense of the whole experience had led her to real evil—communicating with spirits, reaching out to the spirits of dead people, and, eventually, opening the door to demons through her relationship with the false guardian angel.

When Christina returned home, the ministry continued, and healing came slowly over many, many months. Some prayer sessions were done by phone. During the healing process, Christina's mother had a dream and heard a voice say,

"I can have one member of the family in every generation." She also heard the words "unholy shroud" and "unwrap her." Christina and her mother called me for prayer, and I asked Christina's mother to act on these words.

As Christina's mother lifted her hands as in a mime, unwrapping invisible bandages from Christina's body, Christina described a physical sensation to me: "From the top of my head, down I feel this tight binding being slowly unwrapped."

In separate incidents during our ministry to Christina, two people saw in their minds an image of a woman holding a baby in a hospital nursery. Both people felt uneasiness, much like Janelle's experience of creeping fear. The team began to ask the Lord to reveal what this meant for Christina's freedom and understanding. He revealed, as Christina testified, that it was "someone—a nurse or employee in the hospital where I was born, probably—doing a ritual of witchcraft over me as an infant." Yet, God, through the ministry of prayer teams at Aslan's Place, set her free.

Chapter Two

THE MINISTRY OF DELIVERANCE

I N 1989 WHEN Donna and I took our first tentative steps
into deliverance ministry, our whole church was affected.
For me, especially, it was as if we had boarded a roller
coaster and were climbing that first, terrifying hill.

I remember the wild ride down that hill very well. We
prayed with a few people, and it was like someone released a
memo that read, "Go to this church." People—needy people,
hurting people—started coming from all over, all of them
wanting prayer. So we prayed for them.

A handful of people joined me to pray. God began to heal
and to bring change and hope. For our congregation, our small
team of prayer warriors, and me, this was only the beginning.
People started receiving words of knowledge, even though I
didn't know what that gift was. They started having visions
and speaking in tongues. It was amazing!

Donna and I sought counsel, and I read everything I could
find on the subject of deliverance. Clearly God was delivering
people from demonic oppression, curses, and inner wounds.
As the pastor of my church, I worked hard to maintain the
certainty that my ministry stood on firm biblical ground.

Precept upon precept I outlined a theology of deliverance ministry.

BIBLICAL FOUNDATIONS OF DELIVERANCE

Christians cannot be possessed by demons. We were "bought with a price" (1 Pet. 1:18–19; 1 Cor. 6:20). *Nothing* can "snatch" believers out of Christ's hand (John 10:28). However, Christians can be influenced, affected, oppressed, or hurt by demons. Believers are commanded to arm themselves with spiritual weapons to "stand against the wiles of the devil" (Eph. 6:11, NKJV). We are also told that our battle is not against flesh and blood (ourselves and other people), but against powers and principalities, against the rulers of the darkness of this world, and against spiritual wickedness in high places (Eph. 6:12).

Sin and the curses that come with it affect the family line (Exod. 34:7). However, God allows us to repent and receive forgiveness and cleansing for our sins and the sins of our ancestors (Lev. 26:40). Jesus taught His disciples (and all believers) to pray for their own spiritual protection and deliverance. His words in what is commonly called the Lord's Prayer literally mean "deliver *us* from the *evil one*" (Matt. 6:13, emphasis added).

Jesus and the apostle Paul ministered deliverance and spoke openly about it. In Luke 11:20 (NKJV), Jesus said, "I cast out demons with the finger of God." He sent demons into pigs (Matt. 8:29–32). He delivered people who asked for physical healing (Luke 4:40–41) and at least one person who didn't ask (Luke 4:35). Paul simply commanded, "In the name of Christ…come out of her," and demonic spirits of divination left a girl (Acts 16:16–18).

The unique authority given to believers in Jesus' name

includes authority over all demons (Luke 9:1; Mark 16:17), authority over all the power of the enemy (Luke 10:19), and authority to pull down strongholds (2 Cor. 10:4). Believers are instructed to "resist the devil" (James 4:7); the stated result of this resistance is that "he will flee from you." If, as some teach, Christians cannot be affected by the demonic, this instruction would be unnecessary. Although God is the source of power to deliver, He chooses to use humans to accomplish this (Luke 10:17).

Establishing a sound biblical foundation for deliverance ministry is critical, and many people approach deliverance with a Bible in one hand and a stack of books in the other. As good as knowledge is, however, the time comes when theory and theology must be put into practice. Many biblically grounded, effective models and approaches to deliverance ministry exist.

After thousands of hours learning, studying, testing, and asking the Lord to show me how to effectively pray for deliverance and spiritual freedom, it became apparent that the spiritual universe is as infinite and complex as the physical universe is. I could grasp the idea of one, holy, creator God; Satan; angels; and demons; but what about everything else? What about spiritual ties to birthplaces, generational sin, or corporate sin of nations and peoples? What about those odd references to principalities and powers in Ephesians or to the princes of Persia and Greece in the Book of Daniel? What is the point of trying to learn about deliverance ministry if the spirit realm is so far beyond human understanding?

My conclusion is that the Lord gave us one model of prayer for deliverance. It is not a method or formula to follow, and it isn't magic. It doesn't address everything required for deliverance, but it is simply one approach to help bring people to new levels of spiritual freedom. God doesn't reveal every need, source of brokenness, or generational curse at once. He often shines the light of His Holy Spirit on one issue at a time, bringing deliverance gradually.

I will always be growing, learning, and waiting on the Lord. My perspectives or practices might change as God increases my understanding through the hands-on process of praying for wounded people, yet deliverance prayer must always be empowered by the Holy Spirit. The spiritual weapons of the blood of Jesus and God's Word are available through the authority Jesus gives His people. Like a messenger carrying the king's signet ring, each Christian carries, speaks, and acts with the authority of our King, the Lord Jesus. The model below applies these principles of God's Word to deliverance ministry.

A SIMPLE MODEL OF DELIVERANCE

Form a prayer team with at least two other believers. As you begin to minister, ask the person who is receiving ministry to pray a prayer of renunciation. The following is an example:

> *In the name of Jesus Christ and by the power of His blood, I cancel any oaths, covenants, agreements, rituals, or spells made against me with or without my will. I break any pronouncements against me by any familiar spirit and any spirit connection. I repent for any generational sins in my family line from the beginning of time to the present. By the blood of Jesus I cancel all curses resulting from generational sin. I ask for God's blessings for my children and my children's children to a thousand generations.*

Ask the Holy Spirit to come and minister to the person. Ask the Lord Jesus to reveal any past event that created an opening for the enemy. Does the person have any thoughts, memories, or dreams to share? If so, ask the Holy Spirit to confirm what is true. Sinful actions toward or against an individual can wound and make a person vulnerable to demonic attack and harassment. An individual's own sin actually creates an open door to the enemy. Ask the Lord to reveal what sin gave opportunity to the enemy.

Address the issue of generational curses. Sin affects descendants to the third and fourth generation and, in the case of illegitimacy, even to the tenth generation. Since sins can be repeated in each generation, a generational curse can continue through numerous generations. If there is no repentance and forgiveness for sin, it carries a curse. Inner wounds weaken the spirit, allowing patterns of sin to continue generation after generation. The result is a generational curse.

Ask the Lord to reveal any generational curse and seek to learn how many generations back it was first empowered. Then ask the person to renounce, repent of, and ask forgiveness for any sin committed in the family line. This is called identificational repentance. Ask the Lord Jesus to cover the family line and the memory or incident with His blood. Pray that He will break all ungodly connections from that event to the present. Also pray that all ungodly ties will be severed between it and the person receiving prayer and his or her own children.

Demand that all evil leave and go wherever Jesus commands it to go. And, finally, end the session with prayer for the cleansing and protection of the Holy Spirit over the person who has been receiving ministry, the prayer team, and all family members. Instruct the person who has received ministry to maintain personal discipleship and accountability in the church or through a mentoring relationship.

The Exercise of Spiritual Gifts

A couple in their sixties came to me for prayer because the wife's deep emotional pain and struggle had driven them to seek help. In their mainline Christian church, no one ever breathed a word about deliverance. Prayer, like everything else, was expected to be *orderly*. They came to the prayer session feeling frightened, reluctant, and suspicious.

As I opened the prayer session, I asked, "Lord Jesus, what are You doing today? Is there a memory that You want to bring up from the past? A dream or recent experience?" The room was silent. Nothing happened. I prayed again. Nothing.

Then I noticed an expression of intense concentration on the husband's face. When I asked what was happening, he indicated that he was seeing something in his mind: a little girl huddled in the corner of a room. His wife made no reaction and was without emotion, but the man began to weep."

Thus began a fascinating interaction in which the husband saw, felt, and experienced emotions and memories long-buried in his wife's mind and heart. He saw a mental picture of his wife as a little child being ridiculed by her mother. As her husband was flooded with feelings of condemnation, loneliness, and rejection, the wife stared straight ahead, still without emotion or seeming recognition.

What was happening? The wife truly trusted only one person—her husband. In her life, only he had expressed unconditional love to her, and despite this man's suspicions about deliverance and the prayer time, God used him as the primary tool to bring desperately-needed healing to his wife.

As God's purpose in the prayer session unfolded, both husband and wife received freedom and healing. The wife gradually opened herself to the pain and emotional wounds she had kept buried. The Holy Spirit revealed long-forgotten memories. Generational sin was addressed. Deep wounds and roots of sin, called demonic strongholds, had made the woman vulnerable to demonic harassment. These bonds were broken and the demons evicted.

At the same time, in God's gracious economy, the husband also found freedom. His spiritual gifts were revealed and unwrapped. He was used in ways he had never dreamed possible, and the Lord brought him into a new spiritual realm.

This prayer session was not unique. In session after session, our prayer teams see the Lord release spiritual gifts. People begin to hear God speak. As we ask questions, we receive answers. Using yellow legal pads, team members record words, information, images, or whatever they sense. Individual team members compare the impressions and information they have discreetly written during the session to confirm "by the testimony of two or three witnesses," each one acting independently of the other, that a given message is of God (Deut. 19:15; 2 Cor. 13:1).

We have found that a pattern emerges during prayer. Often, as mentioned above, two or three prayer team members receive the same information, image, or word. A shared Scripture will be met with nods of confirmation. A team member might feel intense fear, shame, anger, or other emotion, only to hear the person receiving prayer express that exact emotion. A recurring image might be perceived visibly or in a team member's mind. For example, someone once heard in the spirit the words, "Closet…ask about a closet," and asked the person receiving prayer, "Does a closet mean anything to you?" The person who was receiving ministry began to weep and described, in detail, the childhood memory of being locked in a closet by a teacher.

I have long believed in the gifts of the spirit, and I had taught for years that we were to use our spiritual gifts to minister to others. Now I have seen them revealed and used in ways I had never imagined. This has brought great joy to my heart. Each prayer session becomes a hothouse of spiritual activity, and each person with different gifts helps to set a person free. Intelligence, education, occupation, or position in the church are no longer factors. We come together unified in submission to our Lord and in compassion, waiting on Him to see how He will use us. Finally, here is an extraordinary exercise of spiritual gifts that are working together for the common good.

Chapter Three

THE FUNCTION OF
SPIRITUAL GIFTS

S OME CHRISTIANS HAVE difficulty accepting the use of spiritual gifts—especially gifts like tongues, interpretation of tongues, prophecy, healing, words of knowledge or wisdom, and discernment—because they seem more supernatural, and even peculiar. Gifts like mercy, teaching, intercession, or exhortation may seem more natural and commonplace and, as a result, less worrisome or discomforting. We expect to see Christian brothers or sisters teaching, encouraging each other, or acting with mercy; but we do not expect to hear prophetic words spoken casually in the church social room or words of knowledge shared during a Saturday morning men's breakfast.

However, appearances can deceive. The natural gifts are not more or less God-ordained or God-given than the more esoteric gifts. Scripture clearly teaches that all spiritual gifts are distributed among God's people as part of our Father's great plan and purpose. (See 1 Corinthians 12:7.) All gifts are appropriate for use in prayer ministry. It is also necessary to balance freedom in response to the Holy Spirit with sensitivity to the differing perspectives, theology, or just plain discomfort of others.

Of course, not all spiritual gifts are used in every prayer ministry session or by every prayer team. However, I consistently find that God keeps His promise to supply all our needs by giving gifts when and where they are needed. Let's take a look at the spiritual gifts that are commonly manifested in prayer ministry and see how they function.

HEALING

As C. Peter Wagner has explained, believers who receive the God-given gift of healing "serve as human intermediaries through whom it pleases God to cure illness and restore health" by divine and miraculous rather than natural means.[1] God, of course, is the power behind healing. Yet, in His amazing plan to use human beings for His glory, people to whom He gives the gift of healing are truly His hands and feet. Although every Christian can pray for healing, some individuals are uniquely gifted by the Lord for this ministry.

We should not expect God's gift of healing to appear in a particular form. Even though our Lord was absolutely perfect, He loved showing incredible creativity; for example, He rarely healed the same way twice. He used physical touch when He healed the severed ear of the high priest's slave (Luke 22:51). When He healed a deaf-mute, He acted symbolically, using His fingers to plug the man's ears and then place His saliva on the man's tongue (Mark 7:33). In His healing of a man who was blind from birth, He made mud with His saliva and rubbed it on the man's eyes (John 9:6).

Nonetheless, Jesus merely spoke to the paralytic, saying, "Take up your bed, and go to your house" (Luke 5:24, KJV), and the man was instantly healed. In Matthew 8:13, He spoke and the centurion's servant was healed, even though the servant was miles away and never personally asked for healing. A woman was healed by touching Jesus' clothes and later, as recorded in Acts 5:15, people received healing as Peter's shadow fell on them when he passed by.

Scripture offers a somewhat overwhelming banquet of possibilities to anyone who is seeking a biblical model for healing. As we consider the vast array of ways God may heal, our Western, rational thought is challenged—perhaps to the point of unraveling—by the fact that Jesus healed a blind man by spitting on dirt and applying the resulting mud to the man's eyes. Words like *disconcerting*, *confusing*, and *faith-stretching* leap to mind.

With Scripture as our model, we can expect the gift of healing to manifest in diverse ways during prayer ministry. Someone exercising the gift of healing may speak aloud. He or she may read or proclaim a verse or section of Scripture over the sick. Some believers routinely touch the person who is receiving prayer. Others act or move symbolically. After a prayer session, one woman wrote scriptures recounting God's promises and power to heal on bits of paper and slipped them into her son's shoes and clothing.

Many diseases, though certainly not all, have a demonic root. For example, sometimes Jesus healed the sick by addressing the physical illness. Sometimes He commanded demons to leave. In chapters 2, 5, 7, and 8 of Mark's Gospel, Jesus addressed physical illness directly, and the people were healed. In Mark 9, a desperate man brought his sick son to Jesus. Today medical science might describe the boy's ailment as epilepsy, but Jesus ignored the physical illness and commanded demons to leave the boy.

TONGUES

The gift of tongues is speaking to God in a prayer language not learned by the speaker and/or the ability to receive and communicate a message or word from God in an unlearned but divinely-anointed prayer language. During prayer ministry, it is sometimes a weapon in spiritual warfare. Prayer in tongues may open the heavens, allowing a breakthrough for insight or the release of power. Speaking in tongues may bring greater freedom and ability to hear God instruct, command, give information, or reveal truth and lies about a person's life and family line.

INTERPRETATION OF TONGUES

The interpretation of tongues is the God-given ability to translate an unknown prayer language to bring understanding to what the Lord is doing and saying in prayer sessions. Two team members with the gifts of tongues and interpretation often function in tandem, the first receiving a word in tongues and the second receiving the interpretation.

MERCY

Mercy, according to Wagner, is "the special ability God gives… to feel genuine empathy and compassion for individuals, both Christian and non-Christian, who suffer distressing physical, mental, or emotional problems and to translate that compassion into cheerfully done deeds that reflect Christ's love and alleviate the suffering."[2] Although mercy is often a quiet, gentle gift, God can use it powerfully in prayer ministry.

At times a team member with a strong gift of mercy is able to clearly see into the heart of the person receiving prayer and understand deep pain or emotional wounds where other team members only see the resulting anger and defensive behavior. Sometimes the gift of mercy is expressed in sympathetic or symbolic actions. Prayer team members sometimes weep. Some seem to know exactly what to say or do to bring comfort or encouragement.

Once when team members from Aslan's Place gathered for open ministry during a church conference, a teenager asked for prayer. The young man crumpled to the floor, his chin resting on bent knees and his expression flat and emotionless. The team began to pray.

Nearby, another young man began to weep, bent over in pain. The prayer team asked the Lord about him and received immediate, consistent answers that he had the gift of mercy. He was feeling the emotional pain his friend couldn't feel. The team leader beckoned and the young man tentatively placed his hands on the first boy, who was overcome with weeping at that very moment.

The gift of mercy was a critical part of the healing Christina received in the story of her deliverance in chapter 1. "The prayer sessions were so intense," Christina said, "and I was exhausted and overwhelmed. Donna Cox has the gift of mercy. She would always know when I needed a break. She'd fix tea and listen and love me. That was a huge part of my healing."

Any time a spiritual gift is used in prayer ministry, the gift and the gifted person must be submitted to the counsel and discernment of the team and the team leader. For example, our prayer teams have learned that people with mercy gifts can be too protective of those who are receiving prayer. Sometimes the gentle, loving expression of the gift of mercy must be restrained to allow the person receiving prayer to fully experience and grapple with his or her own pain and emotions.

DELIVERANCE

Deliverance, says Wagner, is "the special ability that God gives…to cast out demons and evil spirits" for the purpose of freeing individuals from demonic influence and effects.[3] Individuals with this gift speak and act with marked authority in deliverance ministry. It is helpful, perhaps even essential, that prayer team leaders have received the gift of deliverance. A leader with this gift will guide and direct the prayer team and ministry with God-given authority.

Sometimes an individual with the gift of deliverance is unusually aware of a demonic presence or influence. During one prayer session in Wisconsin, a woman who was receiving prayer shared a terrifying dream in which she was a nine-year-old girl who was being chased down a long hallway by a "man wearing black clothes…just a shadow and no face." During the dream, which occurred repeatedly, the man ducked into a room to hide.

The woman tried counseling, prayer, and the use of Scripture to set spiritual boundaries, but the dreams continued. She asked the Lord to explain what her dream meant, yet there was no answer. Who was this faceless creature?

Finally, the breakthrough occurred when a prayer team leader with deliverance gifts stepped in. Armed with the authority of Jesus' name and His blood, she bound the demonic presence to the will of Jesus and commanded it to be silent. "You will speak and act only as the Lord Jesus Christ permits," the leader commanded. "You will leave and present yourself before the true Lord Jesus. You are forbidden to return."

The dreams stopped, and the woman began to receive insight and specific scriptures to help her understand the dreams. She began to hear God speak again. The debilitating fear faded and left. In time, she was ready for deliverance ministry.

INTERCESSION

Intercession is the God-given ability to pray for an extended period of time on a regular basis and see frequent and specific answers. Individuals with the gift of intercession pray with power and consistently receive answers to those prayers. Intercession is both the act of lifting needs before the Lord and warfare prayer characterized by spiritual authority and use of the whole armor of God in spiritual battle (Eph. 6:10–18).

The prayers of gifted intercessors are critical to prayer ministry, both inside and outside prayer sessions. Isaiah 62:6 calls intercessors "watchmen." Intercessors do keep watch. They watch for the enemy and call on the Lord with such determination that they "give Him no rest" (Isa. 62:7).

Intercession is sometimes paired with the gifts of discernment, mercy, and prophecy. In a prayer session an intercessor may receive direction or words from the Lord or may spend the entire time in silent prayer. In either case, the intercessor plays a key role on the ministry team. Intercession can turn the tide of spiritual warfare and deflect the lies and deception of the enemy. Gifted intercessors are both a first line of defense, as well as a spiritual "advance team" that prays through obstacles and listens attentively to the Lord for direction and spiritual insight.

Teaching

The gift of teaching, Wagner explains, "is the special ability that God gives to certain members of the Body of Christ to communicate information relevant to the health and ministry of the Body and its members."[4] This gift is more than the ability to communicate well or to speak articulately. Men and women with the gift of teaching often receive direction from the Lord about what teaching is needed by a church, group, or ministry team. God gives a unique ability to understand spiritual truths and principles and a corresponding ability to pass this understanding on in the form of clear, scripturally-grounded teaching.

Teachers prepare people to give and receive prayer ministry. When a gifted teacher lays a foundation with clear, biblical instruction, everyone benefits. Team members learn how to effectively answer questions and explain biblical principles. People who receive prayer gain confidence as they understand what is happening and why.

In ministry, teaching gifts are sometimes paired with gifts of knowledge and/or wisdom. In prayer sessions, a member with the gift of teaching may explain relevant biblical truths and principles with particular clarity or apply Scripture in a way that brings understanding and insight. Sometimes God uses teaching gifts prophetically by revealing the exact scripture that speaks to an individual situation.

Faith

According to Wagner, the gift of faith is marked by "extraordinary confidence [in] the will and purposes of God for the future of His work."[5] It extends to confidence in the Word of

God, His faithfulness, and the dependability of His promises. Faith is often partnered with other gifts. For example, an individual with the gift of healing may demonstrate unusual faith in praying for the healing of others. Someone with the gift of discernment may pray with boldness and confidence that others do not share when the team is asking the Lord to reveal truth.

In deliverance ministry, the gift of faith encourages the team and pushes members to greater faith. A team member with the gift of faith may encourage others to persevere in spiritual warfare or to continue in prayer, believing that the Lord will act and bring what is needed.

EXHORTATION

The word *exhortation* comes from the Greek root word that means "comfort."[6] As Wagner says, the spiritual gift of exhortation is given by God so the recipient may "minister words of comfort, consolation, encouragement, and counsel to other members of the Body in such a way that they feel helped and healed."[7] Many who come for prayer are discouraged, crushed, and hopeless. They are desperate for comfort, encouragement, and new direction in their lives. Exhortation, like laughter, is good medicine—just what the doctor ordered.

Sometimes, when prayer sessions seem to reach an impasse, faith and exhortation join hands to build up and encourage. Especially at the end of prayer sessions, many individuals feel overwhelmed and in pain. After feeling the devastation of the past and seeing some of the generational pollution in their family lines, people are lifted up by a gifted exhorter bringing the precious comfort of the Lord and His guidance and encouragement for the future.

KNOWLEDGE

Knowledge, in the words of Wagner, is "the special ability God gives...to discover, accumulate, analyze and clarify information and ideas."[8] God often uses this gift as He works through a prayer team. I will discuss this further in chapter 4.

WISDOM

Wisdom, according to Wagner, is the God-given ability to "know the mind of the Holy spirit."[9] The gift of wisdom gives insight, allowing believers to understand and apply God-given knowledge. I will talk more about this gift in chapter 5.

PROPHECY

"The gift of prophecy," Wagner says, "is the special ability God gives to certain members of the Body of Christ to receive and communicate an immediate message of God to His people through a divinely anointed utterance."[11] I will discuss this gift in greater detail in Chapter 5.

DISCERNMENT

Discernment, Wagner explains, is the God-given ability to "know with assurance whether [events or behavior] purported to be of God are in reality divine, human, or satanic."[10] Chapters 6 and 7 are devoted to detailed teaching about this gift.

Chapter Four

GOD'S PROBING REVELATIONS

A WORD OF KNOWLEDGE is information or under-standing received from the Lord. In prayer ministry, the word of knowledge is usually received *for* or *about* the person receiving prayer. We see an example of this in Chris's story.

Late in the year 2000, Chris came for prayer with a laundry list of issues, pain, and physical and emotional strug-gles. He was in a black hole of depression and needed healing and deliverance. In his despair, he was self-abusive, and he described himself as a cutter, the name often given to people who cut their skin as a means of expressing emotion. During his prayer session, he spoke of a "dark place" and said, "I am always there. Always alone."

The Lord spoke clearly to Beth, one of the prayer team members, and told her, "Ask about the closet." When she obeyed God and asked Chris about this, he began to wail, "My teacher locked me in the closet. I don't remember why. Sometimes I was there all day. How did you know about the closet? How *could* you know?" Chris wept and wept. "That's when I started to cut myself," Chris whispered.

In John 4, Jesus' word of knowledge led to the salvation

of the Samaritan woman. This story shows how Jesus defied cultural and religious norms by conversing with a Samaritan woman. As they spoke, He confronted her about her statement that she had no husband and said, "You are right when you say you have no husband. The fact is, you have had five husbands, and the man you now have is not your husband" (vv. 17–18).

The woman was undone. No human being had told Jesus her shameful secret, yet Jesus didn't reveal this secret to shame the woman as a liar and adulteress. He revealed the truth because she couldn't be free or whole until she acknowledged her sin. Jesus showed that the function of the word of knowledge is to separate truth from falsehood and its intent is to bring salvation and deliverance.

In prayer ministry, God sometimes gives words of knowledge to reveal information, facts, or insights the prayer team doesn't—and often couldn't possibly—know. Words of knowledge can provide critical direction and understanding. Like signs on a busy freeway, they tell prayer teams when to move more slowly or quickly, when to exit, and how to pursue an issue or direction. In Chris's prayer session, God revealed information the prayer team couldn't have otherwise known because Chris needed to revisit those memories of the closet to receive healing.

Like the Samaritan woman, people are often shocked by words of knowledge. Like Chris, they wonder, "How did you know? How could you know?" In response to this question, the prayer team member explained, "How did I know? I didn't. But Jesus knew. He never left you." God used a word of knowledge to open Chris's spiritual eyes. In His economy, words of knowledge are given both for the prayer team and for those receiving prayer ministry. While they give direction and insight to the prayer team, God also uses them to break through denial, fear, repressed memories, or self-deception in the person receiving prayer.

GOD REVEALS TIMELY PRINCIPLES

Scripture records in Acts 10 that the apostle Peter received a word of knowledge and describes how that word was used for ministry. In a vision Peter saw animals lowered to earth in a giant cloth and heard a voice say, "Get up, Peter. Kill and eat" (v. 13).

Peter was appalled. Some of the animals were unclean by Jewish law, and he had never disobeyed God by eating pork, carrion-eating birds, shellfish, or other unclean flesh. Yet, the voice commanded, "Do not call anything impure that God has made clean" (v. 15).

After the vision Peter was confused. What was the meaning of it? While he was still trying to sort through the images and words he had received, three men knocked at the door. They were servants of Cornelius, a well-known Roman official and a God-fearing Gentile. Peter was about to learn that his vision was, in fact, a word of knowledge given by God to provide critical information he would need to respond to these men.

Miles away, Cornelius had been praying when an angel appeared with instructions: "Send…for Simon, who is called Peter" (Acts 10:32). Cornelius not only dispatched his servants to find Peter, but he called for his entire family and close friends to hear what Peter would say. God had set up a real dilemma for Peter. Would he jump at an invitation to share the good news of Christ with spiritually hungry people? Normally, yes. But Cornelius was a Gentile. By Jewish law,

Peter could no more enter a gentile home, sit at their table, share their food, and speak to their women than he could eat pork. The entire situation was unclean—and forbidden.

But God had given Peter a word of knowledge at exactly the right moment. He had given him a vision that revealed a principle: who was he to call unclean what God Himself had called clean? God had prepared Peter to see Cornelius and the men at his door as He saw them, as spiritually hungry human beings, clean and beloved in His sight. Obeying the word of the Lord, Peter went with the men, and in the end Cornelius and the whole crowd that was with him heard the gospel message and believed. God poured out the Holy Spirit on them and they praised God in tongues. An amazed Peter baptized them all.

During the early 1990s, I received a prophetic word of knowledge that would change my whole ministry. A friend, a prophet in North Pole, Alaska, called me and said the Lord had told him to give me Matthew 8:16: "When evening came, many who were demon-possessed were brought to Him, and He drove out the spirits *with a word* and healed all the sick" (emphasis added). My friend said, "You will speak a word—even a single word—and the enemy will leave."

At that time I, as well as our prayer teams, always used the same approach to confront and remove demons in prayer ministry. I addressed each demon with authority, demanding and recording every name, "rank," and assignment. (God has also since instructed me to obtain information only from Him when I exercise my authority in Christ to command demons.) Deliverance took hours. Under a surface issue like impatience the team might find demons driving the person to anger, and beneath that layer the Lord might reveal a demonic stronghold of fear and a deep root of abuse or abandonment. Sometimes demons created spiritual obstacle courses to slow the process and mislead the team.

Deliverance was like peeling a spiritual onion, never knowing what demonic strongholds were hidden under each layer of pain or hurt. Therefore, after my friend's word of knowledge, I knew what I had to do. With some reservation, the next time I had a prayer session I simply said the word *leave.* An amazing thing happened. I could feel the demonic leaving.

At first it seemed confusing that my friend would give me Matthew 8:16, a specific Scripture that seemed to be taken out of context. However, in the Lord's exact, perfect time, I understood that God used it as a word of knowledge to provide critical information to change my ministry. He wasn't setting down a rule or instructing me never to say more than a single word or always to say *leave.* He was revealing the principle that Jesus had given authority to His bride in such abundance that demons do not have to be battled one by one. Believers can command and demons will flee.

TESTING WORDS OF KNOWLEDGE

The word of knowledge, like all spiritual gifts, is a powerful tool that must be tested. The Lord instructs us to test every spirit when we receive any information or leading in prayer ministry. (See 1 John 4:1.) Although the focus of this chapter is on testing words of knowledge, the principles and practices I discuss here apply to testing input from prayer team members who operate in any spiritual gift.

To test a word of knowledge means that we ask the following questions:

- Is this word consistent with Scripture?

- Is the information given consistent with God's true nature?
- Does the information given lead the prayer team to greater understanding or specific direction?
- Has the Lord given unity and agreement to the leaders and prayer team concerning this word?

God uses such questions as traffic lights. They line the route of ministry and signal us—if a red light, to *stop now*; or if a green light, to *keep going*.

During prayer sessions a team member may receive a word of knowledge through an inner sense or an audible word. Some prayer teams write these words down and pass them to the team leader. It is often immediately apparent whether a word lines up with Scripture.

Team members who consistently receive applicable, scriptural information should be encouraged to pay close attention to thoughts, impressions, words, or phrases they hear in the spirit; to audible, specific Scripture verses; and to both visible and spirit-perceived images. An emerging, maturing gift should be guided by and submitted to the team and to a mature mentor, pastor, or leader.

A word of knowledge that is confirmed by the person receiving prayer can be a green light. We look for answers to questions like: Is the word true? Did this event really happen? Is the information accurate? Does the person who is receiving prayer say, "Yes, that's exactly what happened," or "That's how I feel. How did you know?"

Words can also be confirmed in other ways. Before one prayer session in Minnesota, an intern strongly sensed that the woman receiving prayer was so emotionally and spiritually broken that she was "in pieces," without a stable core personality. At the start of the session, the woman herself received a word of knowledge. "I see a glass bowl," she reported, "but it's in a million tiny pieces. Pieces are all over the place. I know it's a beautiful bowl, but it's so broken that you can't tell." Such confirmation was a bright green light.

Testing requires communication. During ministry sessions, a team member might receive a word of knowledge and slip me a note that describes it. As a leader with gifts of discernment and wisdom, I may realize the word is accurate, but the timing is off. I may test the word with a team member who is known to have the gift of wisdom or the ability to see what is occurring in the spirit realm. I may encourage an emerging gift of knowledge by saying, "Thank you. Let's ask the Lord about this." At the same time, I will keep the prayer time focused by communicating, "The Lord is working right now. This word might be for later. Let's wait and see what the Lord says."

When Red Lights Flash

A red light flashes when a team member is unwilling to learn from mentors, consistently struggles with leaders, or insists on the rightness of any input. A word of knowledge, like any gift, should be *submitted* for testing rather than *presented* as authoritative. Even the most gifted and mature can be mistaken or deceived. One purpose of team ministry is to bring all gifts to the table as everything is tested with the Holy Spirit. In time, some individuals demonstrate a track record that confirms their gifting. Sometimes gifting is formally confirmed, prayed over, and released in the church or ministry team.

Red lights also signal danger. Individuals must guard their

attitudes and motives; they must be willing to fail and willing to have their words tested. As I have noted above, questions like the following facilitate testing: Do you automatically expect yourself or others to receive a word of knowledge? Do you assume that what you hear in the spirit is accurate? On the other hand, do you assume that you probably won't receive a word from the Lord? Do you disregard what you hear in your spirit?

Sometimes a red light flashes *because* of our good intentions. Faithful prayer warriors desire to hear the Lord correctly and respond to His leading. However, that very motivation holds the potential for error. I once ministered with a seasoned deliverance minister who had prophetic gifts and received words of knowledge. However, I was shocked by the degree to which this man influenced the direction of the prayer sessions. It was dangerous. Some people are so visual that if you ask a direct question, they immediately visualize it and can be influenced to believe it actually happened to them.

Asking the right questions in a prayer session is important. For example, asking, "Does the word *boat* mean anything to you?" is quite different than saying, "I see a boat. Did anything happen in a boat?" Asking, "Do you have any specific memories from age five or six?" allows a response without suggesting what it should be. On the other hand, asking, "Were you touched by a man with a beard when you were little?" may actually pressure a person into finding a memory that never happened. Like a skilled attorney, prayer ministers must probe and inquire without "leading the witness." Mature teams avoid leading questions or comments.

Donna and I once had the privilege of ministering to three generations of one family. The parents had been missionaries in New Guinea during the children's growing years. One motivation for seeking prayer was their son's constant struggles with sexual sin. Lust, pornography, and infidelity had driven his marriage to a crisis point.

During a prayer session, one team member received a word of knowledge in the form of a vision. She saw a child being taken into the jungle and heard the Lord speak in her spirit that the child was three years old. She told me privately what she had seen, but I felt we shouldn't reveal anything without further confirmation from the Lord.

At the next prayer time, the man still had no relevant memories of his childhood. I looked at his wife and sensed that she would see what had happened to her husband. She did have a vision of little boys being taken into the jungle by men who performed an idolatrous ritual over the boys and sexually abused them. This opened an unrelenting demonic attack against the man, and healing began only when the team broke the demonic stronghold rooted in the event.

Differing gifts emerged in the prayer ministry to this man. The Lord first revealed a word of knowledge to open the gates of healing. However, God used my wisdom gifts to caution, "Wait for confirmation." Then He gave a prophetic word to encourage the man's wife to speak.

It could have been tempting for the team to plunge ahead in response to that first, clear word of knowledge from a gifted leader. Directive questions like, were you abused in New Guinea? or, do you remember being taken into the jungle as a little boy? would have sidetracked the entire process. The team might easily have missed the Lord's plan to speak through me in prophecy and through the wife with a powerful, confirming word of knowledge.

In Chris's story, which I shared at the beginning of this chapter, Beth, the prayer team member who received the word of knowledge about the closet, felt timid and hesitant to speak.

"If I'm wrong," she thought, "I could detour or confuse the direction the Lord is taking. I don't want to suggest anything to this person that might not be from the Lord." Such second-guessing can be a red light cautioning us to slow down. On the other hand, the Lord might be saying, "Don't assume you aren't hearing Me. Share what you have received with your team."

Consistent errors and input that is "off" are cause for concern, but a mature prayer team can be trusted to test and discern. Missing the mark or making a mistake isn't a disaster. Mistakes happen. Hearing God's voice has potential for the same mistakes as human communication.

Imagine a family workday out in the yard and the voice of your spouse calling, "Hey! Need a break?"

"How thoughtful," you think. "I really do need a break." You grab a couple of sodas from the fridge and meet your sweet, sensitive spouse on the front sidewalk. With a huge smile you say, "Just what I needed, a break!"

"Break? What break? I said I needed a *rake*," your spouse grumbles. With a good dose of grace, you may remember that your spouse is still the same, thoughtful sweetheart you smiled at ten seconds earlier.

Yes, mistakes happen. Beth received an accurate, literal word of knowledge about a closet. But accuracy and literal-ness should never be taken for granted. Just as *rake* could be mistaken for *break*, the word *closet* could have been symbolic instead of literal. It could have referred to a hidden wound or secret. It could have been a signal that Chris was hiding the truth. It was possible that in Beth's genuine desire to help, she convinced herself Chris's "dark place" was a closet. Beth had to risk being wrong and trust her prayer team's discernment, wisdom, spiritual maturity, and ability to test the accuracy of her word.

Expectation can be another red light. A prayer team shouldn't assume, "She always gets a word of knowledge," or "He'll hear the Lord for the direction we should take." Such expectations can pressure team members to perform and open the door to deception. When one member often receives accurate words of knowledge, the team can lean too much on that *person* instead of waiting on the Lord. Another pitfall can be neglecting to test words because a trusted, mature member of the team receives them.

Chapter Five

WORDS OF WISDOM
AND PROPHECY

S PIRITUAL GIFTS RARELY stand alone in ministry. In *Discover Your God-Given Gifts,* authors Don and Katie Fortune have grouped words of knowledge, words of wisdom, and prophecy under an umbrella of "gifts of perception."[1] These gifts are not only differing facets of a single gem, but they are often closely related and even interdependent. Thus, this chapter will follow the preceding teaching on words of knowledge with instruction on words of wisdom and the gift of prophecy.

As I mentioned in chapter 3, C. Peter Wagner defines the gift of wisdom as the God-given ability to "know the mind of the Holy Spirit."[2] In prayer ministry, the gift of wisdom gives insight to understand and apply God-given knowledge. This gift was very important in the prayer team's ministry to help Christina on the journey to spiritual freedom in the story presented in chapter 1. As I mentioned there, it became clear to Janelle, one of our team members, that Christina's spiritual friend was neither a guardian nor an angel, but an actual spirit being—a demon that held her in bondage.

Knowing this information was helpful, but knowing what to *do* with it was the critical next step. Should the team rebuke and cast out the demonic intruder? Was it first necessary for Christina to repent and break agreement with the demon and the relationship? Was Christina able and willing to sever the relationship?

As I prayed and asked God what He wanted to do, He gave me clear instruction concerning the direction and process, and He promised to remove the demon. However, Christina had opened a door by agreeing to the relationship, and she needed to renounce and sever the relationship by her own free will.

I spoke directly to Christina with compassion and spiritual authority and asked, "Are you ready to know the truth about your guardian angel? You must tell your guardian angel to present itself to Jesus and then ask Jesus Himself to reveal the truth." After an intense, inner struggle that lasted more than twenty minutes, Christina did as I directed her. She asked the Lord to reveal whether the guardian angel was wearing a mask, and the beautiful face of her companion slipped away, revealing a hideous demon.

In this incident the prayer team worked well together. The Lord used those with gifts of discernment to confirm that Christina's angel was, in fact, a demon. Then the Lord showed me through words of wisdom how to apply that information. In simple terms, God spoke with words of knowledge or discernment to reveal what was happening. Then He communicated through words of wisdom to reveal what to do in response.

A striking biblical example of the gift of wisdom in action is the well-known story of the adulteress in the eighth chapter of John's Gospel. Religious leaders hoped to use this woman, caught in the act of adultery, to trap Jesus between the just requirements of the law and His own message of mercy and forgiveness. Jesus, however, didn't take the bait. He affirmed the rightness of the law without denying the wrongness of the woman's sin. He looked the religious leaders in the eye and said, "He who is without sin among you, let him throw a stone at her first" (v. 7, NKJV).

What a powerful example of the spiritual gift of wisdom! Jesus clearly understood the facts: the woman was an adulteress who deserved stoning according to God's Law. No doubt Jesus understood much more about the woman—and her accusers. However, the facts only showed what was happening. Wisdom showed how to respond.

TESTING WORDS OF WISDOM

As with any gifting, prayer teams must test and provide accountability for wisdom gifts. They should regularly ask "green-light" questions: Is this consistent with Scripture? Is the team in unity? Does it confirm this?

One red light in the exercise of wisdom and other spiritual gifts in prayer ministry might be called "no formulas." Godly intentions can be detoured by relying on what worked before. Recalling that Jesus never seemed to use His gift of healing in the same way twice, prayer ministry teams must remain flexible, open, and willing to change at the Holy Spirit's prompting.

Another red light is reliance on natural gifts. Some people are blessed with an extra measure of human wisdom and just plain salt-of-the-earth common sense. These wonderful folks always seem to clean their rain gutters and balance their checkbooks. Count on them to ask the practical questions, plan ahead, and keep their not-so-practical brothers and sisters on schedule and within the budget. However, human wisdom and common sense must not be confused with the God-given spiritual gift of wisdom.

Human wisdom functions in the natural world, relying on logic, information, careful evaluation, and reason. In contrast, a God-given word of wisdom is a spiritual exchange. Our part is not to reason, deduce, or solve problems. Operating in the gift of wisdom requires that we wait for the Lord to speak and direct. His wisdom might or might not reflect common sense.

Like every positive trait, human wisdom is a dim reflection of the Father's own character and nature. However, while human wisdom is consistent and logical, a God-given word of wisdom could easily contradict every leading that is based on logic and reason. Words of wisdom must be tested, of course. A challenge for prayer teams is to set aside human wisdom and reason and measure the words received against the plumb line of Scripture and the carpenter's level of unity.

PROPHECY: A TIMELY WORD

As I wrote in chapter 3, Wagner has explained that the gift of prophecy is given to the body of Christ "to receive and communicate an immediate message of God to His people through a divinely anointed utterance."[3] Don and Katie Fortune define prophecy as "an anointed proclamation of God through an individual to encourage, exhort, or comfort."[4] And in his book *Prophetic Etiquette*, Michael Sullivant describes prophecy as both foretelling (proclaiming what God plans and will do) and forthtelling (revealing God's heart, intent, and purpose whether in the past, present, or future).[5]

Prophetic gifting is a precious, powerful tool in prayer ministry. I once had a four-part dream the night before a deliverance prayer session, and the next day I realized the dream was a prophetic blueprint. Each time the team reached a "what's next?" point in the session, the Lord would remind me of the next part of the dream.

Sometimes God sends prophecy to move prayer teams to a new level of maturity. In 1990, with our deliverance ministry expanding by the day and team members experiencing manifestations of the Holy Spirit, my congregation grew increasingly uncomfortable. Disagreement seeped into the leadership, and some church members simply wanted the whole strange thing—and me—to go away.

About this time, Linda, who eventually became a trusted intercessor for Aslan's Place, showed up at the church office with a prophecy that the deliverance ministry would grow. She said that I would be used to set many free and to train many others. She ended by saying, "The Lord sent me here and said this is going to happen to you. Pretty soon you will be traveling all over the world."

My first thought was, "No. None of this is going to happen." Then the Lord sent T. L. Fairley, a seasoned prophet to further stir the pot.

Donna and I invited Brian and T. L. Fairley to dinner at our home. Of course, as a pastor, I had to show off the church, but when T. L. walked into the sanctuary, it was like a tractor beam grabbed her and dragged her to a pew. She sat down and said, "Deception sits here." As she started weeping, I wondered what in the world was going on. Then I watched in astonishment as T. L. walked around the sanctuary prophesying, "What is happening here is going to affect this church, this region, this state, this country, and the world."

Over the next months, the Lord drew the Fairleys and Donna and me together. We would be on the phone three, four, five times a week between our homes in Los Angeles to San Diego. She would give me prophetic words and scriptures, and she had dreams and visions. I had a stack of prophecies she gave me, and nothing happened with any of them—until the conclusion of my time as pastor of the church.

The words God sent through Linda and T. L. seemed improbable, even ridiculous. Yet they were confirmed as they occurred. The ministry that began with a skeptical pastor teaching on spiritual warfare spread and spread like ripples in a pond. As the Lord had said, invitations came to minister and teach: first in California; then in other states; and finally at churches, conferences, and to groups of Christians in Asia, across Europe, in South America, and New Zealand. Donna and I took our insights and anointing for deliverance across the region, the country, and the world.

In prayer sessions God will sometimes give prophetic words that say, "This is what I'm going to do," or "This is what I have done in the past." He may use a prophetic image to release someone from years of rejection and emotional emptiness, as he did for a man in Vienna. This man described his life as having been "crippled by rejection," and he had no self-esteem. He was so overcome by the lie that the Lord couldn't love him that he couldn't hear the Lord's truth. As I was praying for him, I heard the Lord say, "He is the son of the King. He has worth that no one can take from him."

Immediately the story of King David and Mephibosheth in 2 Samuel 9 came to my mind, and I spoke the prophetic word to him. "You are the son of the King," I said. "You have worth that no one can take from you." I recounted the story of Mephibosheth, the son of Jonathan and the last living descendant of King Saul, who was crippled from the age of five because he fell from his nurse's grasp when she was fleeing after the death of Saul and Jonathan. (See 2 Samuel 4:4.) Historically, new kings safeguarded their thrones by wiping out the former royal family to the last member, but David sought out Mephibosheth.

David honored Mephibosheth with a place at the royal court—not because of anything Mephibosheth had done, but because he was of the king's family. "Mephibosheth was crippled," I observed, "so David had him brought to the table, where no one could see his legs. His scars and shame were covered. He was honored because he belonged to the royal family, a status no one could take from him."

God used this prophetic image to release the man from the rejection he had suffered for years. Like David honored Mephibosheth as part of the king's family, God restored this man to his rightful position—equal before everyone and, more than equal, a royal descendant. In prayer we applied this principle, and suddenly that man understood who he was in Christ.

TESTING PROPHETIC WORDS

It is a challenge to test prophecy that foretells what God intends to do in the future. I tested the prophetic words of Linda and T. L. Fairley by waiting until they occurred. However, not all situations allow this luxury. Prayer teams must learn to hold "future" words lightly, like a driver cresting a hill with an intersection on the other side. The driver knows the intersection is there, but it is unknown if the light will be green or red. Wisdom says, "Slow down. Be prepared to stop. Pay attention. Look for signs."

If a prophetic word is given with an attitude of insistence, that is a red light. As is true with any spiritual gift, prophecy must be submitted for testing with open hands. Even when a team member's gifting is consistent and strong, the team must not assume that a word is accurate.

Another red light is the action of assuming when and in what form a prophecy will occur. A danger, even when a prophetic word is accurate, is that individuals act on the prophetic word in their flesh instead of waiting until the Lord reveals and creates His perfect way and time.

Linda and T. L. Fairley both received prophetic words that Donna and I would take our ministry across the world. However, I didn't start collecting names of international leaders in deliverance ministry so I could introduce myself and arrange meetings. Rather, I went right on ministering, waiting, and doing what God set before me.

In time, doors began to open: a request to speak in an area church, a phone call from a ministry leader in another state, a meeting with leaders in deliverance ministry. Each open door led to another. The challenge for Donna and I and their prayer team was to walk through each opened door and wait for the next whether it seemed to lead toward the prophecy or away from it.

Chapter Six

DISCERNMENT OF
GOOD AND EVIL

A S A PASTOR, I was accustomed to being around hurting people. They wept in my office as they poured out stories of confusion, abandonment, and betrayal. My pastor's heart longed to help, but often I could only refer them to therapists for counseling. Sometimes they got better. Sometimes, they didn't.

In the late 1980s the Lord began to reshape the ministry He had given Donna and me. His call on our work and our lives was that we would minister deliverance. In the process, God dismantled our expectations, revived and renewed our understanding of spiritual gifts, and generally remodeled our theology and vision of the body of Christ. When I, along with others, began to pray for people, spiritual gifts lit up all over, just as if the Lord had hit a heavenly switch.

A group of earnest intercessors and prayer warriors came together, and they reported strange, out-of-the-box experiences. Their theology was shaken in the presence of words of knowledge, visions, and prophetic words. Of course, they were to test every spirit, but faced with actual spirits to test, no one knew what to do.

During ministry sessions I asked team members to write down impressions, words, or visual images they received. I thought that the Holy Spirit would confirm by giving the same revelation to more than one person. Along with our prayer teams, I tentatively followed the Holy Spirit into the unknown territory of spiritual warfare, testing spirits, and manifestations. We continued to pray, and people received healing.

All this time, I didn't feel, hear, or see a thing spiritually. Nothing. Then I began to feel a peculiar pressure on my head during some prayer sessions. I approached T. L. Fairley, who often saw physical manifestations of angels and demons, and said, "I'm feeling this pressure, what do you think it is?"

"Well, I'm seeing demons," she responded. With that information, a slow process began by which the prayer team members and I grasped what was happening in us and our ministry. Team members reported unusual, unexpected, physical sensations like nausea, shaking, pressure, pain, or tingling. Not everyone had such experiences, and among those who did, the reports were as varied as the people reporting them. I stumbled upon the realization that when prophetic team members said, "There's a demon here," I experienced physical pressure on my head.

During a prayer session for a woman diagnosed with dissociative identity disorder, the woman began to speak. "Paul, the Lord says, 'Do you want to see her healed?'"

"Yes, Lord," I answered.

The woman began to recite a whole series of prayers canceling the power of demons and witchcraft. A tingling sensation like an electric current hit me with physical force and swept across the top of my head. As it passed, I felt great joy. I was stunned. "Could that sensation be a response to the presence of the Lord?" I wondered. I, along with my partners in ministry, entered a period of testing and growth. God was about to reveal the gift of discernment in its varied, intense power and mystery.

TRAINING YOUR SENSES TO DISCERN GOOD AND EVIL

Most Christians have been taught that the gift of discernment allows believers to examine natural or spiritual actions, events, doctrines, or practices to determine whether they are good or evil. They have also been taught that discernment is the God-given ability to determine whether a spirit is godly or demonic.

Although these understandings are biblically accurate, failure to address the means by which discernment occurs has left many believers to rely on an intellectual process of analysis and application of scriptural truths and principles. Within this understanding, discernment becomes merely skilled decision-making or the ability to weigh evidence and deduce answers.

The Bible identifies discernment not as a human ability, but as a spiritual gift.

> Now to each one the manifestation of the spirit is given for the common good. To one there is given…the message of wisdom…knowledge…to another faith…to another gifts of healing…miraculous powers…prophecy, to another *distinguishing between spirits.*
>
> —1 Corinthians 12:7–10, emphasis added

The New King James renders the gift of discernment in the above passage as "discerning of spirits." Elsewhere it is translated "discernment of spirits" (NRSV), and "distinguishing

of spirits" (NAS). In the New Living Bible this text is para-
phrased as "the ability to know whether it is really the Spirit
of God or another spirit that is speaking."

As I sought understanding of this gift, I received a call
from Dr. Tom Hawkins, a scholar and Dallas Theological
Seminary graduate involved in ministry to severely abused
people. He said, "Paul, the Lord gave me a word of knowledge—and you know this almost never happens to me. He
gave me this passage, Hebrews 5:11–14. I believe it is a chief
passage for what is happening to you."

I opened the Word and read the following.

> We have much to say about this, but it is hard to
> explain because you are slow to learn. In fact, by this
> time you ought to be teachers, you need someone to
> teach you the elementary truths of God's Word all
> over again. You need milk, not solid food. Anyone
> who lives on milk, being still an infant, is not
> acquainted with teaching about righteousness. *But
> solid food is for the mature who, because of practice, have
> their senses trained to discern good and evil.*
>
> —Hebrews 5:11–14, emphasis added

The final words shone like a floodlight and revealed that
mature believers are ready for the solid food of "teaching
about righteousness." It described one route to maturity with
the statement, "The mature who, because of practice, have
their senses trained to discern good and evil."

For more than a year, we who served on the prayer teams
had struggled with questions about physical sensations we
experienced. Why did one member's hands get numb when he

prayed? Why did another feel pain in her chest? We had experienced smells like rotting garbage, high-pitched shrieking sounds, heat, cold, physical discomfort, and even laughter. We had asked the Lord more than once, "What does this mean?" We were finally on the verge of finding some answers.

Discernment is not child's play. It is a mark of the mature Christian. According to 1 Corinthians 12:10, discernment is a spiritual gift. But as the writer of Hebrews clearly teaches, this gift must be developed by constant practice. Only then will it become a sharpened weapon of spiritual warfare. Only then will God's people become acquainted with "teaching about righteousness" in this area of discipleship and training in godliness.

This made sense to our prayer teams. After all, teachers review notes and practice presentations. Everyone in every field gains maturity through practice. Why should we assume that spiritual development is different? As I told the prayer teams, we too often immediately assume that if we can't do a spiritual activity correctly the first time, what we're doing must not be of God. However, Hebrews 5:14 says that practice is necessary. We're to practice the use of our *senses*. The goal of this practice is to train our five physical senses to distinguish between good and evil.

Evangelicals commonly teach that discernment is an intellectual process of analysis and application of biblical principles leading to logical conclusions, yet the writer of Hebrews, it seems, flies directly in the face of that understanding. Discernment is described as a *sensory* rather than an intellectual process.

How can this be? Although some translations, including the NIV, render Hebrews 5:14 as "train themselves," the Greek is most accurately translated as "train (or exercise) their senses."[1]

The text refers specifically to the five physical senses of touch, hearing, smell, sight, and taste. The writer of Hebrews is saying that discernment operates through the physical senses. It is tested with the mind by rightly applying Scripture.

This insight completed the jigsaw puzzle that allowed us to understand the things our prayer teams were sensing. Our team members have had physical reactions to the presence of demons, angels, witchcraft, spiritual powers, and authorities. They have smelled sulfur and rotting garbage. I have heard the Lord speak my name. I have worked with people who have heard the Lord speak audibly, angels sing, demons talk and laugh, and the sound of horses' hooves thundering by.

IS SENSORY DISCERNMENT SCRIPTURAL?

Throughout history many of God's people have experienced both a godly and a demonic presence with their senses. Even a cursory reading of Scripture reveals a consistent pattern.

God's voice was heard by Adam and Eve in the garden (Gen. 3:8), by Abraham (Gen. 12:1), by Moses (Exod. 19:19), by Joshua (Josh. 1:1), and by Samuel (1 Sam. 3:4). After Jesus was baptized by John the Baptist, how many people heard the voice of God say, "This is my beloved Son, in whom I am well pleased" (Matt. 3:17, NKJV)? This event was of such importance that it was recorded in the Gospels of Matthew, Mark, and Luke.

When Jesus commanded demons to identify themselves in Mark 5:9, they said, "My name is Legion...for we are many." The text indicates the demons *replied*, or said that to Jesus. Therefore, it is logical to assume Jesus *heard*.

God's people see into the spirit world. He appeared to Moses in the physically real though symbolic form of a burning bush (Exod. 3:2). He used an angel to appear and speak to Abraham (Gen. 18:1–2), and He showed himself to Joshua as an angel with a drawn sword (Josh. 5:13).

Scripture also records how evil has manifested itself in physical forms, seen in the natural realm. In Exodus 7:10–12, wooden staffs were transformed into snakes both by God's power and the occult magic of Pharaoh's magicians. God's power was good, and the magic of Pharaoh's servants was evil. However, the results of both were visible in the natural world.

Both good and evil appear in visions. The prophet Isaiah saw the Lord in a vision rather than with his natural eyes, and he described it in detail: "I saw the Lord seated on a throne...the train of His robe filled the temple. Above Him were seraphs, each with six wings: With two wings they covered their faces" (Isa. 6:1–2). As recorded in Revelation 13, John saw Satan (or a manifestation of the enemy's evil) in a vision. He described "the beast" in vivid detail.

The following scriptures record experiences of taste. The Old Testament prophet Ezekiel and the apostle John, the writer of the book of Revelation, each received a vision in which they were given a scroll to eat. Ezekiel wrote, "So I ate it, and it tasted as sweet as honey in my mouth" (Ezek. 3:3). John received a scroll from an angel. He wrote, "It tasted as sweet as honey in my mouth, but when I had eaten it, my stomach turned sour" (Rev. 10:10).

The Bible rarely refers to a spiritual presence or spiritual realities being perceived through smell. Paul writes of the "aroma of Christ," the "smell of death," and the "fragrance of life" (2 Cor. 2:15–16). Are these poetic metaphors, or is Paul referring to actual smells with which mature—and discerning—believers were and should still be familiar? In addition, Revelation 5:8 and 8:4 describe bowls of incense.

The smell and visible smoke of incense appear to be a physical manifestation of the prayers of the saints.

Both good and evil are revealed by touch in Scripture. In 1 Kings 19, the prophet Elijah fled from Queen Jezebel. Hungry and despairing, he lay in the desert and prayed for death, but an angel of God prepared food and touched Elijah to wake him from his exhausted sleep (v. 7). Peter saw, heard, *and* felt an angel. Acts 12:7 records that an angel bathed in light appeared to Peter, "struck Peter on the side" to wake him, and said, "Quick, get up!"

In Mark 9, evil manifested itself physically in a young boy who was possessed by what Jesus identified as a "deaf and mute spirit" (v. 25). The moment the demon saw Jesus, it "threw the boy into a convulsion" (v. 20). This passage should be carefully noted. Western reasoning would lead to the logical conclusion that this boy suffered from a biochemical/neurological imbalance, resulting in epilepsy. However, Jesus operated in discernment as well as human logic. Although He recognized physical illness elsewhere, here He named and took authority over demonic spirits.

The teaching of Hebrews 5:14 became alive in our ministry and, coupled with confirming Scriptures, established the foundation our prayer teams use to share, examine, and test our sensory experiences. The "solid food" of discernment did produce fruit of greater maturity as our prayer teams grew in confidence, authority, and trust in the power of God's living Word. As they began to understand and use discernment, this gift emerged as an important weapon in the battle for deliverance, healing, and spiritual freedom.

Chapter Seven

THE PRACTICE OF DISCERNMENT

A S PRAYER TEAMS mature, sensory experiences will occur because the Lord gives spiritual gifts to equip His warriors. Prayer ministry is spiritual warfare, and discernment is a valuable weapon, a gift from the Lord that flows from an anointing. This anointing can be sovereignly given by the Lord or passed from one person to another under the direction and power of the Lord. The apostle Paul, for example, wrote to the church at Rome and said, "I long to see you so that I may impart to you some spiritual gift to make you strong" (Rom. 1:11).

Receiving discernment gifts is the first step. Then we put on training wheels and practice, practice, practice. In time, confidence is acquired and we become steadier in the exercise of the gift. The importance of practice is underscored in the experience of Janelle, a member of the team that ministered to Christina in the account I presented in chapter 1.

DISCERNMENT THROUGH TOUCH

Janelle is an active prayer minister whose discernment gift operates through the sense of touch. "At first the sensations were really faint," she says. "We were in the mountains, in an area where a lot of occult activity occurred, and I said 'I think I feel something.' But it was so slight that I wondered if I was making it up. In time and with practice I began to be more sensitive."

To test what she was experiencing in prayer sessions, Janelle compared her physical sensations with words of knowledge, prophetic words, or discernment received by others. She sometimes experienced an irritating, itchy sensation, as if part of her body had gone to sleep. If a team member commented, "I hear the word *witchcraft*," or "I'm seeing a dark cloud of witchcraft over our heads," Janelle made a mental note. Sometimes she experienced the itchy sensation if a scripture about witchcraft was read.

As time passed, the witness of others confirmed that Janelle was discerning the presence or activity of witchcraft through her physical senses. With practice, her understanding and use of discernment grew. She sometimes experiences nausea in the presence of demons. On a recent visit to the vicinity of former concentration camps in Dachau and Schongau, Germany, she was so nauseated she could barely function.

Beth, a prayer minister whom I introduced in chapter 4, has described a physical sensation "like a sharp awl being driven into the small of my back" when witchcraft is present. She sometimes experiences a rotting garbage smell in the presence of demons, particularly those of lust or violence. In the presence of demons of control and deception, she sometimes feels a weight on her chest and finds herself gasping for breath.

Aslan's Place team members have felt chest pains that indicate heartache and labor pains when God is birthing a change. They have felt cold and heat radiating from people's bodies. On occasion God has come to burn away sin or demonic strongholds, and the biblical "furnace of the Lord" took physical form as the temperature in the room rose dramatically. Prayer team members feel shapes, textures, and objects—including scrolls, swords, vases of anointing oil, and pieces of armor—with their hands. Sometimes those who are seers, whose discernment operates by sight, will see what others feel.

I was once invited to the office of a therapist who was counseling a couple. Every time the therapist talked with the husband, she felt as if she had entered a whiteout of confusion. As I stood by them, I could feel a tingling in my hands, and I followed the tingling sensation as a guide. It felt like a wall around the man and was so thick that it extended seven feet from him. Practice had taught me that this tingling signaled the presence of witchcraft. Later the man told me that his former wife admitted to being a witch, and it was very possible that she had cursed him and his new marriage. I realized, once again, that the Lord was teaching me something new.

During another prayer time, a California psychologist felt a box placed in his outstretched hands as I was praying for him. He described the experience this way: "It was as if a beam of light came down from the throne to my office [the psychologist did not report whether this was seen or sensed]… I remember a box that sat on my hands and…in that box were spiritual weapons. I had the sensation that the box shrank and went right into my chest, into my heart."

DISCERNMENT THROUGH SIGHT

Prayer ministers whose discernment gifting is manifested by seeing often start small. At first, shadows or outlines may appear in the natural world or vague images may flash in their minds. With practice, these manifestations may grow in detail and clarity. Some seers may report puzzling, even strange, experiences.

Visions can be detailed and literal. One prophetic intercessor dreamed that a friend's husband appeared in public wearing a dress and fishnet stockings. Not long after, the friend called in great distress to say that her husband was cross-dressing and refused to seek help. Family members didn't believe her and rejected her pleas for help. The intercessor could stand with her friend because the Lord had sent a vision specifically for the situation.

At times, visions are symbolic. During a deliverance session, one team member with strong prophetic and visual gifts of discernment saw television satellite dishes surrounding the woman who was receiving prayer. "I don't know anything about satellite dishes," the prayer minister said. The woman being prayed for said, "But I hear noise all the time. Chatter inside my head. Thoughts and ideas and constant, constant noise."

The team leader immediately prayed, "Lord Jesus, is this Your voice speaking?"

Around the circle, prayer team members made silent eye contact with the team leader, shaking their heads no. The woman blurted out, "No, Jesus is saying that is not His voice."

The team leader acted with authority, forbidding any voice but the voice of the true Lord Jesus to speak and asking the Holy Spirit to reveal the source of the noise. Demons of deception and confusion were ordered to leave and their assignments to create noise in the woman's mind were cancelled.

I sometimes see the effect of spiritual action or beings. Just as the invisible wind causes trees to sway and leaves to fall, the presence of angels or demons is sometimes seen as flickering light, movement, or shadow.

Sue, a church elder who is involved in prayer ministry at a local church, was puzzled when she first began to see in the spiritual realm. Many Christian friends felt uncomfortable with the idea of visions. She had to search for others who shared her experiences and could help her understand and test them.

"Sometimes what I see is symbolic," Sue explains. "I see symbols or patterns." Sue once saw geometric figures and heard in her spirit the words, "What's your angle?" She asked the Lord what that meant and soon understood that a member of their congregation had an untapped gift of discernment. He could perceive whether others' motives and intent were righteous or unrighteous.

Sue sees in the natural sometimes. "Once I saw a fine powder drop from the ceiling during worship," she said. "It expanded like a cloud. I actually felt it on my skin. The interesting thing was that I continued to see the room and people at the same time." Sue often sees symbolic images with her eyes, like a ticker tape with words written across it, playing cards, fire coming from someone's fingers, trap doors, or snares.

Seers must test what they see. Skeptics may suggest that mental pictures and images are imagined or the power of suggestion at work. Those same skeptics may dismiss images perceived with the physical eyes as hallucinations. Scripture validates visions perceived by the mind and visions seen in the natural world. However, testing is still critical. An image could be the imagination of a well-meaning believer, and recalling Pharaoh's court magicians turning their staffs into snakes, prayer teams must remember that not all physical manifestations of power are from God.

Visions can be tested by asking the Lord to reveal their source. Once, while ministering in an Atlanta home overlooking a beautiful forest, I noticed a hawk circling and then settling on a nearby fence. An hour later, I noticed that the hawk hadn't moved. When I commented about this to the prayer team, only one other person—a seer—could see the bird. I asked the Lord to reveal the source of the vision and an immediate sense of evil swept through the room. In response, I commanded the hawk to leave, and it vanished.

Discernment Through Hearing, Smell, and Taste

Discernment operates through the sense of hearing much like it does through the senses of touch and sight. Experience and understanding tend to start small and grow with practice, just as Hebrews 5:14 indicates. Discernment through the sense of hearing is sometimes symbolic and sometimes literal. Some words or sounds are heard only in the spirit and others are perceived audibly.

Spiritual activity sometimes manifests itself as sound. For example, I hear witchcraft as a high-pitched whine. Once, as I was seated at my desk, I heard an audible voice whisper my name. I walked toward the door and felt pressure on the left side of my head. My hands and shoulders got hot. In the past, I had felt this pressure and heat in the presence of angels. The pressure was very hard, and that happens when there is a message. My wife Donna received a prophetic word that was brought by that angel.

The Lord often speaks directly into the mind. A California pastor was praying over his church building when he discerned two demons standing between the bathroom doors.

"Stupid demons," he thought. "They left the glory of heaven to stand between two bathrooms." He discarded this wry observation as his own passing thought until another person in the room reported hearing exactly the same phrases.

One unusual incident confounded even the most skeptical. In an amazing ministry time with a group of deaf believers, I heard wind come from outside, hit the wall, pass through the room and exit the other wall. Everyone in the room heard the wind—including two deaf people.

It is not unusual for discernment in a prayer team to operate through the sense of smell. For some, this discernment begins with a faint scent and grows in clarity or intensity with practice. The presence of the Lord is often manifested by a pleasant smell, perhaps sweet, like flowers or even baking bread. Prayer team members have commented, "I smell the woods in spring," or "It's smells clean, like snow and winter cold."

Prayer team members sometimes smell demons, curses, witchcraft, or other evil. Not surprisingly, discernment of evil through smell is often described as a stench, like vomit, rotting, or burning. Some people smell irritating chemicals, sulfur, or unwashed bodies. With practice, individuals whose discernment gift operates through the sense of smell may learn to distinguish the smells of demonic activity, witchcraft, and curses. Some prayer team members can distinguish between incoming and outgoing demonic activity. One Aslan's Place team member perceives the spirit of poverty by a distinct smell of rancid food.

A pastor in Zurich, Switzerland, asked for prayer because his ministry seemed fruitless and his efforts frustrated. His wife said success seemed always out of reach. A prayer team member had a word of knowledge that the pastor's fruit was being burned up by the enemy. As our ministry in prayer continued, I smelled smoke so strongly that I began to search the house. Something was on fire! My search led me back to the room where the prayer team was ministering to the pastor, and they prayed to release his ministry. When the demons assigned to destroy his ministry were commanded to leave, so did the smell of smoke. Two years later, his ministry was flourishing.

Examples of discernment through the sense of taste are infrequent both in Scripture and our prayer teams' experience. Sometimes taste functions as a word of knowledge, such as a sweet taste followed by the words "taste and see that the Lord is good," for example."

Especially because taste-perceived discernment is relatively uncommon, those in prayer ministry should pay attention to taste sensations that are unusual in quality or timing. If the taste of a particular food or substance occurs during prayer, the team should ask the Lord to reveal its source and meaning. Demonic presence can be perceived as an offensive smell, and in the same way, it might produce a vile taste. Unforgiveness could be manifest as a bitter taste.

One evening I tasted blood so strongly that I went to spit it out. There was no blood, but immediately the name of a ritual abuse survivor, a man who had been forced to drink blood when he was a child, came to mind. I had prayed with him previously, and now I called him and asked, "What are you doing to me?" He said he had cut his finger and put it in his mouth and instantly remembered being forced to drink blood. He had cried out to the Lord, "If Paul really loves me, let him taste the blood, too."

Our Aslan's Place teams have experienced discernment operating through the physical senses as they have ministered internationally. People in Asia are experiencing the same manifestations of this gift as their counterparts in Africa or Central America. The experiences of small-town, American evangelicals parallel those of urban Spanish-speaking Argentineans. God seems to be releasing discernment gifts in similar ways across the globe.

DISCERNMENT THROUGH EMOTIONS

I will weep when you are weeping, When you laugh I'll laugh with you; I will share your joy and sorrow Till we've seen this journey through.[1]
 —from "The Servant Song" by Richard Gilliard

Prayer teams across the globe share similar experiences of discernment through the five physical senses, and some individuals experience discernment through their emotions. Physical senses produce unconscious, internal reactions to external stimuli. In the same way, emotions spring from the unconscious mind in reaction to situations and experiences.

Just as humans don't decide to see the color green or smell pot roast, we don't decide to feel fear or make a conscious decision to experience joy. Christian mental health professionals are careful to separate emotions from behaviors that are chosen in response to those emotions. Emotions (feelings) are neither right nor wrong. The behaviors we choose in response to those emotions can be godly or sinful.

Mary Ellen, a team leader with a Minnesota prayer ministry, experiences discernment through her sense of emotion. "In the natural I'm sensitive to people's feelings," she says. "In prayer ministry I would often cry, at first in sympathy.

Then it changed. The first time I realized there was something different was when we prayed for a real warrior who has multiple sclerosis. I began to weep. The team was used to me crying, so I moved to the side of the room. At first, the weeping was my heart wanting him to be healed. Then it felt separate from me...as if I were weeping the tears of his wife and daughters. It was more than expressing sorrow; it became intercession, a prayer empowered by the Holy Spirit."

With practice, Mary Ellen's gifting has matured. Sometimes her discernment gift operates through emotions by mirroring others' feelings. At other times, the emotions are symbolic. "We prayed for a woman who had been abused as a child," she says. The team knew that at some point she needed to forgive the abuser, but when my prayer partner began to talk about forgiveness I suddenly felt afraid and lost, like a bewildered child. My body wanted to curl up and hide. I stopped my partner and said, 'Wait, there's a little girl who needs healing first.'"

Prayer team members whose discernment operates through the sense of emotion must learn to separate their own feelings from emotions revealed by the Holy Spirit. These emotions don't belong to the team member experiencing them. Mary Ellen often experiences emotions that the person receiving prayer wasn't allowed to, couldn't, or wouldn't express.

Beth, whose discernment operates through touch and emotion, says, "I test my emotions during prayer. Feelings that are extremely strong, abrupt, or inconsistent with my own emotional personality may be discernment operating. For example, I'm not afraid of men. If I suddenly feel fear when a man enters the room, I ask the Lord to show the source of that fear. Perhaps the person we're praying for has some history of fearing men."

Mary Ellen sometimes discerns the presence of demons through emotions. "I've felt incredible arrogance or hatred," she says. "It seemed to come from nowhere." When demons are present, she sometimes feels an urge to mock or ridicule. Mary Ellen and her prayer team know to take authority over these demons and cancel demonic assignments to hurt the person receiving prayer.

TESTING DISCERNMENT

Is discernment the sole or primary tool of prayer ministry? No. Discernment must be accompanied by other tools and confirmed by team members who operate in other spiritual gifts. When I mentor teams and individuals, I encourage members to share their sensory experiences for testing and teaching. Such experiences must be tested just like prophetic words, Scripture verses that come to mind, words of knowledge, or wisdom insight. This testing is multi-layered. First, the source of the experience must be determined, and then the team must help members discern the meaning.

Testing discernment that is received through the senses requires an attentive, mature prayer team. Healthy skepticism isn't out of line. A prayer team member's palms might radiate heat because a demon is present. On the other hand, perhaps she is nervous or the room temperature is too high. Is the word that is repeating in your mind from the Lord or simply your own, albeit persistent, thought? Is your feeling of sorrow a God-given insight into the heart of the person receiving prayer or is it your own sympathy with a sad situation?

The Lord wants to reveal truth. Teams can ask, "Is this feeling from You, Lord?" or "Father, show us the truth." We can take authority by saying, "We bind any spirit not from the true Lord Jesus to silence," or "If this is deception, we command you to leave." Any discernment must line up with biblical truth and principles. Because Jesus said, "My sheep know my voice" (John 10:4, author's paraphrase), we can also ask Him, "Is that You, Lord?" Again, the team's involvement is critical. Unity is a green light. The Lord will confirm His truth through more than one witness. Confusion and uncertainty are red lights, signaling for us to slow down or to stop because something isn't from the Lord.

Scripture cautions that discernment is for the mature. Prayer teams should see growth in spiritual authority and maturity in members exercising discernment gifts. Ongoing immaturity is a red light. The practice required to train the senses in discernment can actually present a red light of caution. Training takes time. One incident or experience doesn't confirm a spiritual gift.

Every team member must be willing to test discernment, submit to mentoring or accountability relationships, and wait patiently and peacefully while the Lord matures and develops their gifts. When a well-meaning desire to be used by God becomes pushiness, urgency, or insistence, prayer teams should pause and seek counsel from the Lord, intercessors, and leaders overseeing the ministry.

It takes energy and maturity to both train prayer ministers in the exercise of discernment gifts and test what is perceived. Tired, overwhelmed, or emotionally drained team members are vulnerable to confusion and deception. A team's emotional, physical, and spiritual state can be a red light flashing.

Sensory experiences can be powerful and intense. Mary Ellen says that she was drawn to those intense experiences when she began prayer ministry. "There's an adrenalin rush sometimes. I would replay sessions and feelings in my mind.

That wasn't healthy." Mary Ellen and her team recognized this red light, and now they have learned to briefly review sessions and then commit them to the Lord's safekeeping. Some teams include a scribe to release team members from the responsibility of recalling important details.

The principle of discernment operating through the physical senses and emotions is new to some in prayer ministry. Others who have read the preceding pages may recognize experiences they have observed but not understood. Prayer teams should expect and watch for these discernment gifts because God is eager to equip His children for the battle for freedom and healing.

Chapter Eight

THE PRAYER MINISTRY TEAM

Though one may be overpowered, two can defend themselves.
A cord of three strands is not quickly broken.
—ECCLESIASTES 4:12

Every matter must be established by the testimony of
two or three witnesses.
—2 CORINTHIANS 13:1

THE FOUNDATION OF prayer ministry is the living reality of Christ in us, the indwelling Holy Spirit, and the power of God working through and in human beings. Freedom comes because God heals and delivers, not because people are gifted. God can use anyone at any stage of maturity. However, we make ourselves most available to God when we are prepared and disciplined. Experience shows that prayer ministry is most effective when a team of mature believers, knowing and using their God-given spiritual gifts, stand in prayerful agreement and intercession.

C. Peter Wagner writes in *Your Spiritual Gifts Can Help Your Church Grow,* "We are not to operate as lone individuals, but as members of the Body of Christ. When we deal with truths about the spirit world, we look for the agreement of others and we welcome accountability to them for testing the validity of our conclusions."[1]

Earnest individuals who step into deliverance and healing ministry alone will quickly discover the truth that "one may be overpowered." Like wolves that target the deer straggling behind the herd, the enemy of our souls sees loners as easy prey. When our enemy strikes, people are hurt, ministries are destroyed, and whole churches are wounded and torn apart. Sometimes heresy is the tragic result.

When I began deliverance ministry late in 1989, I realized that I was unable to understand what the Lord wanted me to do. Of necessity I invited two or three others to join me. In time a team formed, and spiritual gifts emerged. Team members recorded what they sensed, heard, saw, or received during prayer sessions. Applying the principle of 2 Corinthians 13:1, the team sought agreement of two or three witnesses to confirm information or direction.

People I had pastored for several years began to see and hear from the Lord. As we learned to become a team, I was excited to see how the body of Christ could work together. Each person felt a sense of satisfaction as they were used to help lead a person out of bondage. No person on the team was more important than another. Those who prayed and received nothing from the Lord realized they had still played an important part. At last I saw a real-life illustration of 1 Corinthians 12:7: "Now to each one the manifestation of the Spirit is given for the common good."

In team ministry, each member does receive and contribute, and it is good!

TEAM BUILDING

Teams bring varied gifts and personalities ⌣
of ministry. A team is also a safety net, providing testing, balance, accountability, and discernment. Sometimes leaders build a team with individuals who represent a balance of gifting and maturity. At other times God does an end run around human planning and simply draws together a team of believers with hearts for spiritual freedom and healing. In both cases, the Lord equips the team by releasing spiritual gifts needed for its ministry.

God-given wisdom and insight are required for team building. Not every prayer team member must be a pillar of spiritual maturity and authority. The still-hurting whose hearts and lives are on the mend, who are willing to be mentored and accountable, and who are teachable, often grow into strong, mature team members alongside more experienced brothers and sisters. Mary Ellen, the prophetic intercessor whose ministry I described in chapter 7, says, "When I began, I was still hurting."

PREPARATION FOR FRONTLINE MINISTRY

In 1999 a Wisconsin team formed with a vision of ministering to marriages. Six couples organized, met, and planned. However, their planning didn't include intercession for the ministry. During the month before the team's first weekend retreat, two team members were laid off their jobs and one couple's car was broadsided by a hit-and-run driver. The team coordinator spent Christmas day with back spasms, lying in pain on his living room floor, and two team members contracted severe respiratory infections that dragged on for months.

"We made a serious mistake," the team coordinators said. "Entering into that kind of frontline ministry without intercessors, well, we might as well have worn targets on our backs."

Linda, a staff member at Aslan's Place, has trained and mentored many prayer teams. "Prayer ministry puts you on the front line," she says. "You can ask the Lord to expose your sin, or Satan will do it. Understand that you are going into a battle, and there may be repercussions. Are you solid in your family? Do you have intercessors to pray for you, your family, your ministry, and those dear to you?"

In her work with prayer teams, Linda once saw a promising team falter under the first testing. "They weren't prepared for the spiritual warfare. At Aslan's Place we caution people, 'Don't move in fear, but be aware that there will be attack.'" Teams experience relational conflict, differences in understanding, physical illness, problems with children, car accidents, and more. Sometimes Satan attacks spiritually. Depression, anger, or old, unresolved issues surface. Teams may find that support vanishes as church leaders suddenly become afraid and remove their agreement.

"When someone expresses interest in being involved, I suggest testing with people who know them," Linda counsels. She asks people to apply Psalm 139:23–24, "Search me, O God, and know my heart; test me and know my anxious thoughts. See if there is any offensive way in me, and lead me in the way everlasting."

As the Lord builds a ministry team, each individual enters a process of growth. Janelle, from Aslan's Place, found that she couldn't watch television or read books with certain fantasy or violent themes. As her ministry increased, her need for worship and spiritual feeding also increased.

Mary Ellen, who I mentioned at the end of the preceding section, is a seer whose discernment operates through emotions and sight. She discovered, "What used to be OK, isn't anymore." The more her discernment gift operated, the more she needed to take care of herself. "I had to pay attention to when my body or spirit was tired. If I was exhausted or hadn't been taking care of myself, I became overwhelmed and couldn't stay emotionally neutral," she explained. She came to nurture herself by gardening and listening to music, but learning to trust her team was a challenge.

During one retreat, Mary Ellen and the team had prayed for hours. God used Mary Ellen's discernment gift to connect with and touch people's emotions and woundedness, but in the process she teetered on the edge of exhaustion. "During worship the Lord sometimes shows me the emotional temperature of a group," she recalled. "That night I lost the boundaries between the group and myself. Feelings just swept over me and threatened to pull me under. As soon as that happened, I shut down emotionally. I cried out, 'Jesus, what was that?' His answer: 'That's what can happen, and it can happen with the demonic, too.'"

Growing teams learn to trust and depend on each other. Part of this team's maturing and Mary Ellen's growth was learning how to care for each other. Teams, especially, must be aware of tired, overwhelmed, or spiritually stretched and struggling members. Mary Ellen's team supports her need for time out and holds her accountable to take care of herself physically and spiritually.

PASTORAL OVERSIGHT AND ACCOUNTABILITY

As Aslan's Place trains prayer ministry teams across the globe, I find that pastoral oversight and accountability are key to team building. Ideally, this support would come from a church. However, as Linda says, "If the church can't or won't provide pastoral support and oversight, find someone else. Find another church body or support person. Receiving input beyond the team and team leader is that important. Find someone with whom to talk through experiences. Another pair of eyes and ears will help to test what you're receiving."

Some prayer teams begin because people pray for each other. In the process, they learn about deliverance and inner healing. Individuals grow in freedom and spiritual gifts begin to emerge. One Wisconsin team was birthed when a traditional share-and-prayer-style church house group decided to seek the Lord for prophetic words, anointing, and release into ministry for its members. God responded in power, launching people into teaching, neighborhood evangelism, intercession, Christian media, church leadership, and deliverance ministry.

Teams that are birthed in congregations face special challenges. Some denominations or individual congregations reject spiritual gifts. Church leaders aren't always open to deliverance or inner healing prayer. The manifestation and use of spiritual gifts may be met with alarm or disagreement. Prayer teams could find that the absence of spiritual agreement in the church is an insurmountable obstacle.

Even when a church has caught the vision for deliverance and inner healing prayer ministry, the depth of experience and maturity required may not exist in a single congregation.

The team and church leaders must discern whether mature believers from other congregations should join the team.

If the Lord opens the door to a cross-congregational team, this creates a precious opportunity to build the body of Christ. Bridges of trust and unity can be built when members of multiple congregations join a prayer team or receive prayer ministry. In this situation, the enemy will try to bring disunity and confusion, so leaders must agree upon and clearly communicate the theological and practical foundations of the ministry.

Bringing new members into an existing prayer team is a challenge. Some newcomers are novices who need training and support, while others may be experienced warriors. In every case, however, new members must learn to trust and work with the team—and vice-versa. Newcomers should observe for a time, learning how the team functions together. Experienced team members should mentor each newcomer.

Team leaders must lead by instruction and example. To say, "Well done," is healthy affirmation. However, a team leader can teach, model, and affirm by saying, "I believe the image you saw of a woman alone in the snow was from the Lord. I think it was a word of knowledge that she felt abandoned. Did the Lord give anyone else a similar thought?"

Care and sensitivity are required when immature or needy people want to join prayer teams. Wounded people carrying unbroken curses and demonic influences are like open windows, giving the enemy access. Team leadership includes the difficult task of discerning whether prayer ministry is timely and appropriate for someone. Hurting people and those still harassed and driven by demons must gently be directed to receive more prayer and healing.

PERSONAL HEALING AND TEAM GROWTH

People in deliverance ministry should receive prayer for deliverance themselves. Those involved in inner healing prayer must be aware of their own unhealed wounds and seek prayer when God brings an issue or hurt to the surface. Mary Ellen, who has helped build prayer teams, counsels, "Prayer teams must be intentional about getting their own healing. If you aren't willing to sit in the chair receiving ministry, you're not fit to be on the prayer team."

Team development, nurture, and growth do not happen quickly or by accident. Growth takes time and intentional action. Mature teams regularly ask the Lord, "What now? What do you want us to learn?" One team may, for a time, focus on inner healing. Another may contact prayer mapping ministries to find out what God is revealing about the spiritual atmosphere of its city. Still another team may devote regular time to worship or decide to attend a conference together for renewal.

Teams and prayer ministries must seek out pastoral oversight at all phases of their growth and development. The words *slow* and *grow* are instructive. Take time to get your own healing. Take time to read, listen to speakers and teaching tapes, attend conferences, and learn from others' experiences. Take time to pray and grow together as a team. Some teams invite an experienced deliverance minister to teach and mentor them. Other teams assemble and use teaching resources. For example, Neil Anderson's *The Bondage Breaker* offers solid, introductory teaching. I have created training tapes and videos, and a deliverance manual.

"Remember, prayer ministry is an unfolding process," says Mike, a prayer team leader and pastor. "We don't know the way to go, but Jesus does. Encourage each other. Remind each other over and over, *it's God who does it.* We aren't the answer people. We have the privilege of standing in His authority—in His light—and watching Him do the work of healing."

Chapter Nine

WISDOM FROM THE FRONT LINES

W E WHO ARE in prayer ministry are seeking after the treasures of wisdom and maturity. This chapter will address this desire by offering invaluable insights that have been contributed by seven veterans of congregation-based and parachurch ministry teams to encourage their fellow leaders.

ENCOURAGE AND FEED THE TEAM

Leading a prayer team is like praying for healing. It doesn't happen all at once. You can't make it happen. Wait and watch the Lord do it.

Don't let the team be intimidated by failure. As a pastor, encourage and feed the team. Every member needs a growing walk with God that is vital today. They can't war with yesterday's faith. Make sure they have prayer and emotional support. Be aware. Do they need training? Do they need rest?

Don't get pulled down by seriousness. God is bigger than the ministry. His plan is bigger than deliverance. Bigger than healing. Bigger than spiritual warfare. Deliverance isn't *the* answer. We aren't the answer either.

Remember, as a leader you're a model. Know the team

personally. Pray for them. Remember they are on the front lines, pushing back the darkness. They need to know you're with them.

—M. M., pastor

Articulate What's Happening

As leaders, we lead. Sometimes we pause the session and articulate what's happening. This is teaching and leading. Remain calm. God is in charge. If you're calm, the team will be. I try to model by articulating what I receive from the Lord. I ask that what I receive be tested by others.

I take responsibility for practical things. For example, before the session I rearrange furniture to allow eye contact or get water and tissues.

—M. C., team leader

Communicate Good Standards and Practices

Leaders must communicate good standards and practices.

Take a team member with you when you pray for a member of the opposite sex.

Before you touch anyone, ask permission.

Ask parents' permission to pray with minors.

Do not pray alone. Team ministry is a safeguard for you and those receiving prayer.

Address your own spiritual health with disciplines of

worship, Scripture, accountability, and repentance. Receive the healing and prayer you need to minister.

Never pray demons into yourself. This will not set the person free. Your salvation does not make you immune to demons.

Be accountable. Know when a situation is too complex or difficult, and don't be drawn in. For example, people with dissociative identity disorder or satanic ritual abuse victims need experienced help. Seek professional help when needed.

Take threats of suicide and violence seriously. Individuals at risk of suicide must be referred to professional help. Develop a support team of Christian professionals, pastoral care, and deliverance/inner healing ministry. Sometimes the police and emergency room are part of that support.

Jesus gives authority to command demons. However, many deliverance ministers, including Paul and Aslan's Place teams, do not obtain information from or permit demons to speak. They obtain needed information from Jesus himself.

—L. P., prayer ministry mentor

CALMLY TAKE AUTHORITY

When we prayed with Paul, we noticed how calm he was and how peaceful the sessions were. In other places, we saw rough-and-ready deliverance: demons manifesting, shouting, sometimes people making a big scene. Paul showed us authority born in peace, calm, and being certain the Lord is the One doing the healing. Leaders shouldn't allow demons to manifest and create chaos. Calmly take authority. God is releasing this kind of authority in the body of Christ.

—L. D., Aslan's Place intern

———

Never Work Without Intercessors

In our ministry people are told up front that we are not in the business of ongoing counseling. This is a breakthrough ministry, to move the process of healing along. We encourage people to get ongoing help, if they need it, from a therapist and have a resource group to which we refer people.

We have a director of prayer ministry who receives...calls from persons needing help. She listens prayerfully and decides who should minister to each person. She lines up the team and intercessors to pray during the prayer appointment. Sessions are two hours long. Afterward, the director receives a report, usually via E-mail, of a few sentences summarizing the prayer session. To ensure confidentiality, only initials are used.

I'd suggest the following to any prayer team leader:

- Include a man on the team if a man or couple is receiving prayer.
- Never work without intercessors.
- Leaders should have personal intercessors.
- Don't focus on one method or process. Explore and find out what works for your team. Jesus is our model.
- Leaders need prayer, too. Be humble enough to ask.
- Prior to the session, we send a one-page "what to expect" sheet to those preparing to receive prayer.

- Designate one person as leader during each session.
- Ask the person who is receiving prayer questions like these: Do you mind if we pray in tongues? Do you mind if we place a hand on you gently while praying?
- If team members have unusual gifts, explain them simply.

Prayer ministry is best taught on the job, hanging around with people who are doing it, using your gifts as you can, growing in confidence, and gradually playing a bigger and bigger role on the team.

In 2003, this ministry focused on training. We set up four training classes. Each trainee observed a prayer session. Those interested in joining a prayer team were interviewed and required to go through the steps of freedom outlined in Neal Anderson's *The Bondage Breaker*. Trainees scheduled a two-hour prayer appointment for themselves.

New team members were assigned mentors and invited to attend a ministry fellowship group meeting every six weeks.

I am pleased to say that this has worked. We will double the number of people served this year.

—B. L., director, Midwestern regional prayer ministry

TAKE CARE OF YOURSELVES

Training times are so important. Leaders set the tone and focus. Begin with worship. Let God's Word speak; look at the healing [and deliverance] ministry of Jesus.

Include teaching on generational sin, the importance of the womb, and parents' role in formation of the person. Address forgiveness. Don't assume that people understand this.

Address sexual history. Prayer team members should examine their own. Talk about sex and gender-related issues. Understand and teach the dynamics of abuse. Never forget the power and immediacy of the Cross. Place the Cross between the abuser and the abused. Jesus will take the impact of abuse, the self-hatred, and pain...He will remove the spirit of abuse.

Keep your eyes open for wolves in sheep's clothing. Covens will send people, sometimes without their conscious knowledge, to compromise your ministry and wear you out. They'll send a person who is deeply, deeply needy, whose intent isn't to change but to channel witchcraft and destroy a ministry. If you find yourselves in a situation where one person is a leech, ask God to reveal the truth.

Ask the Lord to reveal appropriate limits, and stick to them. The Evil One will overwhelm you with people and just plain wear you out. Just as a drowning person grabs and pulls you down, hurting, dependent people will try to put you at the core of their lives. Lifeguards stay an arm's length away and push a pole or floatation device into the struggling person's hands. In the same way, spiritually drowning people need Jesus, not prayer ministers. Dependency is a signal to back up so the people will grab onto Jesus.

Finally, take care of yourselves. Guard your daily walk with Jesus. Keep your marriage healthy. Remember, Satan is a roaring lion, waiting to devour us in our weakness.

After ministry sessions, weaknesses you struggle with—things like overeating, anxiety, self-recrimination, or doubt—will tend to surface. You need cleansing and filling. Perhaps relax and have someone read Scripture over you.

Listen to music. Let the Lord soak you. Sometimes after prayer for sexual healing or deliverance, take a long, cleansing bath and listen to worship music. You have given out. Something needs to be put in. Put in godly things.

—A leader of international prayer ministry teams

HAVE THE CONFIDENCE TO WAIT

Deliverance and healing are parts of the whole plan. Persevere until the Lord brings out the root issue. At the root there's a lie someone has believed, an unconfessed sin, or a curse resulting from generational sin. We have authority to kick out the demons, but don't leave the person still hurting from the pain, wound, or sin issue.

Some team members will sense the spiritual temperature of the person [receiving prayer]. However, those very people who have discernment gifts must ask, "Lord is this You or me? Am I being triggered?" As a leader be aware when unhealed issues are being triggered in the prayer team.

Every deliverance team will experience a season when what worked before is no longer effective. Long-term ministries will suddenly hit walls. Keep your eyes on Him. God is the Healer, not the team, the prayer, or the ministry. A situation may look desperate, but we are not to be desperate. The enemy uses desperation.

As leaders, remember that God wants to heal, but He may not use you or your team. It may not be now. Part of leading is having the confidence to wait. Seal up the wounds, end the prayer session, and wait.

Remember, each prayer session is unique. God is coming

just for that situation and that person. The skills we learn and insights God gives are valuable tools. However, don't come to prayer with a plan. God will place the right tool in your hand at the right moment.

—Arthur Burk

Director of Plumbline Ministries, Whittier, California

Chapter Ten

FREEDOM FOR THE CAPTIVES

CHRISTINA AND JOHN

C HAPTER 1 BRIEFLY described God's beginning work of deliverance in Christina's life and told how she and John left Aslan's Place with the first hope they had known in years. "I was a Christian," Christina says, "but a religious spirit had stifled me. I'd been taught that demons can't affect Christians, so when I was attacked, I didn't know what to think or do. In fact, as long as my faith was luke-warm, Satan pretty much left me alone. I was no threat. But when I said, 'I'm yours, Lord, unconditionally,' then the warfare really started.

"During prayer, the Lord revealed a generational sin of witchcraft in my family line that resulted in a curse over my family and me. There were layers and layers of demons. When I asked how long this battle would be, Paul taught me about spiritual warfare. I knew I was a Christian, but I didn't know who I was in Christ. I had no idea I had any authority. He said spiritual warfare was a way of living in the Spirit, a way of living for peace and freedom. I wanted it."

Over the next few years Christina returned to California for prayer. Generational sins of witchcraft required repentance and healing. When Christina severed her relationship with the demon that had wormed its way into her life in the guise of a guardian angel, change and freedom were released. She began to hear God's voice. The nightmares and voices faded and finally ceased.

For years, the idea that something terrible had occurred when she was about four years old had weighed on Christina's mind. "I had no memory of my childhood. None," Christina says. "Paul prayed that God would show me during the night if anything had happened. During the night I had a dream, and when I woke, I experienced a vision. It was like a video before my eyes. In the spirit I saw an oyster shell opening. Inside was a little girl, about four years old. It was me. Then I saw myself in a dark place."

Long-repressed memories of sexual abuse emerged. Fragments of memories Christina had carried her entire life began to make sense. "As Paul said," she remembers, "when generational curses and demons are removed, memories often surface."

As God brought deliverance and healing to Christina and John, they began to pray for others. They spent months as interns with Aslan's Place teams. In Christina's words, "We've never been the same. Recently a friend prayed for us just before we left on a ministry trip. He saw a demonic face look at us, turn right around, and run."

LYLE AND CAROL

Lyle and Carol's lives could have been lifted from the pages of some heartbreaking novel. Lyle's mother sold her body for money, and as a little boy, Lyle, then nicknamed Butch, grew up like the seed planted among thorns (Matt. 13:7). Promise and hope were choked before they had a chance to take root.

Everything, from school, to sports, to friendships gave the message that he was a bad kid—a loser. No good.

When Carol was nine, her mother left the family, and years of abuse, rage, and violence followed. In a life scarred with running away, reform school, and foster homes, Carol numbed herself with drugs and alcohol and careened from relationship to relationship like a car without steering or brakes. She married an abusive man, and into this chaos a child was born.

By the time Lyle and Carol made their way to Jesus, Lyle had spent time in prison and Carol's child had been taken from her. As Christians, they had hope, but both still lived in a constant undertow of hurt and pain.

Carol describes her past daily life as "pain coming out in rage, confusion, and fear. I was tormented by spirits of fear. If I messed up, I couldn't shake the blame. I'd cope and cope until I'd have an outburst of rage. Then the cycle started again. I couldn't read Scripture. I couldn't listen to music for five minutes, especially worship music. I knew I needed God's word, but I'd sit through a sermon and couldn't remember anything. Scripture made no sense. There was constant chatter in my head accusing me, constant thinking that no one liked me."

By 1987 both Lyle and Carol knew they needed deliverance. They searched for any church, conference, or ministry that promised help. In Oregon, God led them to a church with a growing deliverance ministry, and Lyle began to hear God speak. He would receive words of knowledge during prayer but didn't know what was happening or how to express it. Meanwhile, Carol struggled on, tormented by fear, rage, and unresolved pain.

"In 2002 our church elders heard about Aslan's Place," Lyle says. "At that time, a prophetic word was given to us about

Isaiah 22:20, 22: 'I will summon my servant.…I will place on his shoulder the key to the house of David; what he opens no one can shut, and what he shuts no one can open.'"

The elders wanted to check out Aslan's Place themselves before they referred it to others. However, in desperation, Carol pushed through their reluctance and a barrage of demonic lies. "I told our elders I couldn't wait. I said I would call Aslan's Place myself, even though a lie kept repeating in my mind, 'They won't help. They won't call you back. Don't bother.'"

Finally, Carol called Aslan's Place and received the only remaining appointments. God met Lyle and Carol during their prayer sessions with a strong, confirming action. "One amazing part was that two team members received and acted out a prophetic word," Lyle recalls. "They took a stack of dollar bills and laid half at Carol's feet and half at mine. We counted and each stack had 22 dollars…Isaiah 22:22. God was giving us the keys."

Carol remembers her prayer session in detail. "The Lord had given Paul a word of knowledge that I have a birthmark on my hip. That is true. Then he said I had Mongolian background in my family line. We prayed. Team members saw images of people riding, killing, lots of violence. I repented for the savagery in my family line and for idolatry and worship in sex and religious cults.

"I left feeling no different, but I was different. Within weeks people were saying, 'What happened to you? You've changed.' It was true. What used to pull me under didn't have such power. I could mess up and let it go. I wasn't smothered by shame anymore. Now, years have passed, and I can say I really have been delivered."

Lyle received a precious gift of healing during his prayer session. "I always knew there was a broken place in me, but no one had ministered to it. Paul asked if I had a nickname as a kid. I did—they called me Butch. Paul asked, 'What do you see?' and in my mind, I saw myself as a kid, playing baseball. I wanted to make the little league team so much. The coach sent me and another kid out into the field. He hit the ball over my head intentionally so the other guy would catch it and get the spot on the team.

"I could feel that pain. What happened was like a symbol of my life. I'd never felt like a whole, adult person. I always felt like a spectator. Paul asked if I could forgive the coach. It was amazing. I forgave him, and I received such healing. I wasn't a wounded child anymore. Now I see a difference. I relate to peers like I never did before. I don't hide anymore. I'm not a spectator in my own life anymore."

CALLED TO A MINISTRY OF DELIVERANCE

> That I may know Him and the power of His resurrection.
>
> —Philippians 3:10, NKJV

In 1989 I was an earnest but skeptical American Baptist pastor stumbling into his first deliverance prayer session. Since that time Donna and I have taught, ministered to the bound and brokenhearted, and battled for the spiritual freedom of people in many countries. The call to deliverance and inner healing has swept us into a whirlwind of speaking, teaching, and ministry. God has blessed us with amazing, life-transforming experiences of His power to set captives free.

Experiencing the power of God is a wonderful privilege and incredible joy. However, we must never forget the reason for power and gifts: that we might know Him and that others might know Him more fully. Our joy is to help others enter into a more intimate relationship with our Lord and see lives transformed.

When people receive from God's presence and power through our ministry and write letters like the following, I remember why we serve in the ministry of deliverance and the importance of the spiritual gifts He has given us.

> Father, thank You for the incredible transformation You have done and are doing in my life....Yesterday's sermon was from Isaiah 6....You had an angel take a hot coal and touch his lips. Your symbol of judgment touched him where his greatest need was, but instead of bringing him judgment, Your glory and grace cleansed him. That is what You have done for me...for the first time in a long time I didn't feel guilty at church. I could look people in the eye. I didn't want to get out of there as soon as possible.
>
> And more than that, my heart overflowed with joy and worship. For the first time ever, I felt free to stand and lift my hands. I wanted people to... see Your glory and Your grace and what You are doing in me.
>
> Father, I stand in awe of You. All my head knowledge has begun to become heart knowledge. My salvation is truly *mine*. Father, I could say thank You a million times and not come close to

giving You anything in return. I love You. I am in the field and I am experiencing freedom.

This is the reason for deliverance and inner healing ministry. The heart of God touches human hearts, and we long for what He longs for—to see people set free. And God doesn't stop with longing. He places His Word, His blood, and His spiritual gifts into the hands of His warriors as weapons in a spiritual battle. The Holy Spirit enters into the battle with us.

God is raising up deliverance and healing ministry in the body of Christ because He has heard the cries of His people for freedom. He is issuing this invitation to warriors everywhere: Come. Take up your weapons and join the battle. Take up spiritual gifts to bind up the brokenhearted. Proclaim freedom for the captives and release from darkness for the prisoners.

He has anointed us to minister to a world that is longing for freedom. Are you ready? Will you come?

NOTES

CHAPTER 3
THE FUNCTION OF SPIRITUAL GIFTS

1. C. Peter Wagner, *Your Spiritual Gifts Can Help Your Church Grow* (Ventura, CA: Regal Books, 1994), 210.

2. Ibid., 194.

3. Ibid., 97.

4. Ibid., 120.

5. Ibid., 192.

6. James Strong, ed., *Strong's Exhaustive Concordance of the Bible* (Nashville, TN: Thomas Nelson Publishers, 1997), s.v. "exhortation."

7. Wagner, 143.

8. Ibid., 190.

9. Ibid., 120.

10. Ibid., 200.

11. Ibid., 96.

Chapter 5
Words of Wisdom and Prophecy

1. Don and Katie Fortune, *Discover Your God-Given Gifts*, (Ada, MI: Chosen Books Publishing Co., 1987).

2. Wagner, 120.

3. Ibid., 200.

4. Fortune, 15.

5. Michael Sullivant, *Prophetic Etiquette* (Lake Mary, FL: Charisma, 2000).

Chapter 6
Discernment of Good and Evil

1. *Vine's Complete Expository Dictionary of Old and New Testament Words* (Nashville, TN: Thomas Nelson, Inc., 1996).

Chapter 7
The Practice of Discernment

1. Richard Gilliard, "The Servant Song," Integrity Music, Inc., 1977.

CHAPTER 8
THE PRAYER MINISTRY TEAM

1. C. Peter Wagner, *Your Spiritual Gifts Can Help Your Church Grow.*

TO CONTACT THE AUTHOR

Aslan's Place
18990 Rocksprings Rd.
Hesperia, CA 92345

www.aslansplace.com